GR 221 RUTA DE PEDRA EN SEC

SERRA DE TRAMUNTANA

Miquel Rayó, Joan Sastre, Vicenç Sastre and Sebastià Torrens

TRIANGLE POSTALS

© **Triangle Postals SL**
Sant Lluís, Menorca
Tel. 971 15 04 51
triangle@triangle.cat
www.triangle.cat

Text
© Joan Sastre, Vicenç Sastre and Miquel Rayó

Photography
© Sebastià Torrens

Maps and drawings
© Vicenç Sastre

Translation
Steve Cedar

Technical support
Departament de Medi Ambient
del Consell de Mallorca

Graphic Design
Joan Colomer

Layout
Aina Pla

Production
Imma Planas

Printed by
Igol, S.A.

Registration number: B-39889-2008
ISBN: 978-84-8478-356-5

The authors
Each in their own way, the four authors of this
guide are veterans in the business of acquiring
and spreading knowledge about the nature
and culture of the Balearic Islands. With his
photographs Sebastià Torrens has illustrated
books (*Les aus de s'Albufera: la nostàlgia del
fang*; *Natura Mallorca*), magazines, educational
and general cultural materials. Vicenç and
Joan Sastre are authors of *Mallorca vora mar*,
a landmark in the literature of Mallorcan hiking.
The maps, plans and drawings of Vicenç Sastre
are, moreover, frequent in publications about the
Balearic Islands. He is co-author of *Llibre de la
pedra en sec*. Joan Sastre is an expert in paths,
orientation and mountain rescue. Miquel Rayó has
written, among other works, books for children
and young people (*El camí del far*; *El cementiri
del capità Nemo*) as well as texts about nature
(*Cabrera, l'illa sense nom*; *Les basses tranquil·les
d'es Salobrar*; *Mallorca, la Serra*).

▲ **Estellencs**

GR 221 RUTA DE PEDRA EN SEC

The authors and publisher of this book limit ourselves to presenting a route on foot along the Serra de Tramuntana de Mallorca, with some optional, popular climbs to the most outstanding peaks. They are not liable for any event, incident, accident or circumstance that may arise from the use of the information included here. **Some of the The paths described often pass through private property, access to which always depends on the decision of the owners and their agreements with the Consell de Mallorca or other public institutions (specifically the cases of Galatzó, Tomir, l'Ofre, Massanella and Teix, among others).** In any case, ramblers must follow the enclosed path, behave with prudence in the mountain and respect property and the natural and cultural environment.

▲ The Camí Vell from Lluc to Pollença crosses an extensive holm-oak wood

▲ The viewpoint of Sa Dragonera in La Trapa

▲ Rocky spot between Coll des Prat and Coll des Telègraf

ON FOOT
FROM ANDRATX TO POLLENÇA

The Serra de Tramuntana de Mallorca is, as has been said on many occasions, and island within the island. It has also been said that it is the backbone that supports the structure of Mallorca. Both assertions are true to a large extent. The two characteristics make it an undeniably attractive spot: on the Serra is part of the essence of the island. Great landscapes, cosy corners, rural and emblematic historical constructions (the country estates, the castles built on rock, the coastal defence towers, paved pathways) and a very interesting biology.

The Serra protects the rest of the island from cold winds and bad weather, because it detains the storms that come from the west or north. Not all of them, naturally, but most of them. For this reason, the Serra is the rainiest part of the island. Often, on rainy days, the mountains that make up the range appear covered with dense clouds, like a cape, or with snow in winter.

With a length of some ninety kilometres, the Serra possesses the longest long-distance path in the Balearic Islands: the *Ruta de pedra en sec* (Dry Stone Route) or GR 221. We have no hesitation in stating that it is a beautiful path, which will be thoroughly enjoyed, and all of it with fantastic scenery and of great natural interest. It also has the advantage of not being that difficult (although one should still take care).

The Balearic Islands are in the western Mediterranean, facing the Spanish coast to the east of the Iberian Peninsula, south of the French coast and, let us no forget, to the north, and not really that far from, the African coast. In reality they

◀ **The paving of the Camí des Correu, close to Sa Granja**

are two archipelagos in one: on the one hand, the Balearics, made up of Mallorca and Menorca, and on the other hand, the *Pitiuses*, the islands of Eivissa (Ibiza) and Formentera. In both cases, many small and unpopulated islands, islets and rocks emerging from the sea, accompany the larger islands. Here we would highlight Sa Dragonera (natural park, from which we will have splendid views in the first stages of the GR) and Cabrera (national park), as Mallorca's main companions. On many of these isles and islets there are endemic species of lizards, and terns, seagulls and cormorants breed. Ospreys are relatively frequent

▲ **Eroded limestone rocks**

The position of the Balearic Islands has meant that it has been a passing point for navigators and peoples in expansion since Antiquity. Populated for probably 4,000 years, they have constantly taken in cultures and been the object of conquests. The first settlers left colossal monuments, the famous talayots of Mallorca and Menorca, the no less famous *taules* (in Menorca) and *navetes* (in Mallorca and, above all, in Menorca). In the Pitiuses, the Phoenicians left behind many objects (Punic culture). Romans, Visigoths, Arabs and Christians came later. In Palma, the capital, the See, the Exchange and the Castle of Bellver are the great monumental works of Mallorcan history. From the 19th century onwards, Mallorca was visited by many illustrious travellers who produced passionate descriptions (positive or negative, such as that of George Sand, who stayed a few months in Valldemossa in the company of her lover Chopin, the famous composer). In particular, the typical landscapes that captured the admiration of these travellers and which would later turn Mallorca into a pole of attraction of international tourism, are almost all in the Serra de Tramuntana: the Torrent de Pareis, Sa Calobra, Formentor, Valldemossa, Deià, Puig Major de Son Torrella, the Barranc de Biniaraix, the monastery of Lluc…

Today, the Balearic Islands play host every year to millions of tourists and the resident population has reached one million. Due to its smallness and its condition as an island, there is a serious social debate and concern for ensuring balanced development and sustainable regional organisation. It is important that everybody, visitors and residents, and naturally, also the ramblers of the *Ruta de pedra en sec*, thinks about this constantly: they are on an island, in a small environment and with a fragile balance, with splendid scenery, mistreated in some areas, but protected in others, where waste management is a priority, as is saving both energy and resources. We should also remember that the need to safeguard the main Balearic natural spaces has mobilised the local population for more than the past thirty years. Citizens' campaigns and demands have achieved the protection of beautiful spots: Ses Salines de Eivissa and Formentera, Amunts de Eivissa, the south coast of Menorca, with its delightful coves, the lagoon of Es Grau, in Menorca, and, in Mallorca, among others: S'Albufera, Cabrera, Sa Dragonera, Cala Mondragó, Son Real, S'Albufereta, the beach of Es Trenc and Salobrar de Campos, and partially the Serra de Tramuntana itself. All of them are places that are well worth visiting.

The GR 221, or *Ruta de pedra en sec*, runs all along the Serra de Tramuntana de Mallorca, from Andratx to Pollença, and owes its name to a notable ethnological craft: the construction of dry stone walls without the use of mortar, with the stones ordered according to a tried and tested technique. Throughout the walk we will come across examples —original or restored— of constructions raised with this technique: houses, wells, underground springs, snow huts, paths, borders, coalmines, lime kilns, canals, tanks … The Serra has many paths, and this will surprise the rambler doing the GR 221, because there was once intense human activity here, now much reduced: goat hunting, thrushes caught with nets, the search for edible milk mushrooms, archil, reeds and European fan palm, snow, production and obtaining of charcoal, plaster, lime, olives, grazing land (the flocks of sheep from Llucmajor, for example, are brought to the Serra to spend seasons walking along local transhumance paths), etc.

Today, the Serra is, like all the Balearics, a space that welcomes visitors, and that is why one can find lovely little country hotels and rural tourism establishments. Luckily, the big houses, always austere, that lord it over the different estates, are maintained in an emblematic way: Galatzó, Moza, Son Amer (today a refuge on the GR 221), Massanella... And the villages of the Serra have, for being tourist places of interest, lots of services available to the rambler (banks, chemists, transport, shops, bars and restaurants, markets, etc.) and museums and many other points of historical interest, as well as cultural and traditional events: Deià, Andratx, Esporles, Valldemossa, Pollença, Sóller... The gastronomy of the Serra is filling: *arròs brut* (a type of Mallorcan paella), Mallorcan soups, thrush with cabbage, roast kid, suckling pig, snails, *frit de matances* (a stew of different meats and offal)... And the confectionery, really sweet: *ensaimada* pastry, potato cakes from Valldemossa, almond cake, *turrons* or nougats, fritters. For Lent, the sweet or savoury pastry pies, with meat or fish or peas are well worth tasting. Esporles, Banyalbufar, Escorca, Alaró, Selva and other villages in the Tramontana provide local wines that you should get to know. The *herbas dolces* (herb liquor), *seques* (dry aniseed liquor) or *mesclats* (combination of tonic wine and rough brandy) are the most traditional liquors.

The GR 221, therefore, offers a wide range of experiences. As regards walking in the mountain and the discovery of new places, on each stage one can add variants and complementary trips or climbs (some of them, very few, are shown in the guide. However, there is other published material and rambling groups accessible on the Internet, which provide sufficient information). Many walkers are surprised when they are in the Serra: it is a great spot for their sport. There are trips of all kinds and suitable for all levels. Flat with long coastlines. Alongside the sea or more than a thousand metres up. Mountain passes that recall the Pyrenees, humid and sombre holm-oak woods and extensive areas covered with reeds and exposed to the sun. There are also coves where you can have a splash. The landscape of the north Serra leaves no one indifferent. It is beautiful, overwhelmingly beautiful.

▲ Puig de Sant Miquel and Puig de s'Alcadena   ▼ Daybreak behind the Puig de Galatzó

The sea often accompanies us on the horizon, something that enhances the beauty and unique nature of our itinerary. The Serra has coves, cliffs, peaks, mountainsides, ravines, torrents, slopes, paved paths from other times, remains of constructions of traditional use and today of a great ethnological interest, and always with the possibility of making observations of the flora and fauna, without forgetting the geological interest the Serra possesses. On this question, we should remember that the Serra is a place where there are many endemic plants, from orchids through to bushes; and animal species, especially birds, of great ecological interest: the Eleonora's falcon, the Balearic warbler, the Audouin's gull and the grand and spectacular Eurasian black vulture…

The *Ruta de pedra en sec* will not disappoint anyone. We should remember, however, that Mallorca is a dry land dominated by the sun and that the limestone of its mountain is rough and sharp. This means that you should always wear suitable footwear and take plenty of water and a hat. And it is not unusual to find oneself beneath an unexpected downpour or in the middle of a strong wind. Therefore, even in summer, a cagoule and light but warm clothing are a necessity. Maps will also be useful for complementing this guide. A simple compass will enable us to follow some sections with

▲ The genet, very evasive, represents the fauna of the range well

Level of difficulty of the stages expressed in boots

1 boot, very easy
2 boots, easy
3 boots, moderate
4 boots, difficult
5 boots, very difficult

more security as well as to identify more easily the relief that surrounds us. It is also necessary to make an important announcement: in Mallorca, the sense of private property has very deep roots indeed. The rambler must be aware of this and not venture into spots where there are closed gates. You just need to always follow the signposted route of the path. It is also true that the Mallorcan people are very hospitable. In this aspect they are Mediterranean.

It is recommendable not to take dogs, but if you do, they must always be on a lead and controlled. Do not disturb the animals that are grazing (sheep, goats, the occasional ass or mule). Do not light fires under any circumstances, except in spots clearly indicated (one of the great dangers to the survival of the rich ecosystems on the range in Mallorca are forest fires). The path is highly recommendable between October and April. Summer is much harder because of the intense heat, the excessive sunshine and for the dryness. Temperature, sun and lack of water can result in suffocating conditions. Naturally, you need to be in good shape. And if you can, tell someone the route you are taking for each stage. Although it may appear odd, many people get lost in the Mallorcan Serra. Like anywhere else, the mountain of the Serra de Tramuntana de Mallorca is demanding and obliges us to be prudent.

▲ Wren (*Troglodytes parvulus*)

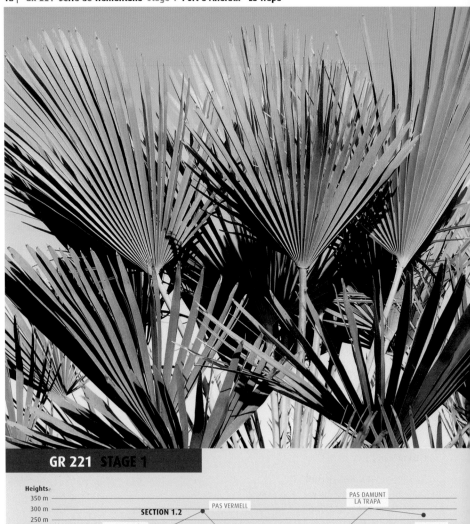

GR 221 STAGE 1

Heights

350 m
300 m
250 m
200 m
150 m
100 m
50 m
0 m

PAS DAMUNT
LA TRAPA

PAS VERMELL

SECTION 1.2

COLL DES VENT

SECTION 1.5

LA TRAPA

SECTION 1.3

SECTION 1.4

PORT
D'ANDRATX

CAN TOMEVÍ

SECTION 1.1

SANT ELM

Distance: 13 km

Time: 3 h 20 min.

Difficulty: easy

Maps:

Instituto Geográfico Nacional 1:25,000 – nos. 697-II and 697-IV

Editorial Alpina 1:25,000 Mallorca Tramuntana Sud

GR 221

3 h 20 mins   Level of difficulty

1

STAGE

1

Departure
PORT D'ANDRATX
Arrival
LA TRAPA

◄ Dwarf fan palm   ▲ El Pas Vermell

The mountain paths of Andratx are a gateway to the past. We discover a world that has not survived the 20th century. The dry landscape shows the scars of the extreme exploitation of human generations and highlights the desire of nature to survive. As far as the last corners we will find the footprint of the diverse cultures that have occupied this land. And we will find viewpoints that will last in our memories, such as Pas Vermell or La Trapa, with the islet pf Sa Dragonera as an inexhaustible photographic object. Andratx will leave us saddened, saddened for what has been extinguished along with the pleasure of still discovering beautiful, still unspoilt corners. At the time of writing the La Trapa refuge is no longer operative.

Key

Road	
Path or track	
Defined path	
Footpath or lane	
Tunnel	
Bridge	
Gate	
Contour lines (50 m)	
Main or minor survey point	
Fissure or cave	
Church	
Cemetery	
Town	
House	
Ruin or hut	
Archaeological remains	
Defensive tower or architecture	
Lighthouse	
Viewpoint	
Municipal boundary	
Canal	
Snow hut	
Car park	
Refuge	
Refuge of the *Ruta de Pedra en Sec*	
Marked route	
Optional route or variant	
Stream or watercourse	
Spring	

Map | 21

1

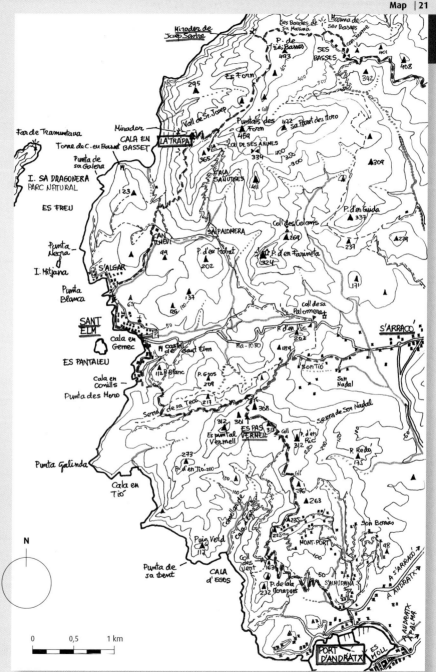

GR 221 STAGE 1	SECTION 1.1 35 mins

FROM PORT D'ANDRATX TO COLL DES VENT

▲ The marina of Andratx

We reach the Port by the Ma-1 road from the town of Andratx, 4 km inland. The old town extends along the right bank of the port. We turn right to pass a bridge over the **Torrent des Saluet**, which drains a salty field with old orchards, with watermills, mills and small cottages. There are still some tamarisks, a typical tree of humid and coastal areas. There are still some boats in the torrent.

We go for some 800 m along Avinguda G. Roca i Garcies until passing before the entrance to the Sailing Club and take the turn towards the right (N), along Carrer Aldea Blanca, which suddenly reaches a junction. The road to the right climbs up to the Mont-port urbanisation. We take the left-hand way (Hotel Mont-port) and after about 300 m we take a turning to the right called Carrer de Cala d'Egües. The asphalt soon ends and becomes a track which, steep and with lots of bends, climbs through the pine wood to the Coll des Vent (163 m). From curve to curve, we come across sections of the old footpath deteriorated by the process of development. Towards the south we see the rocky hill of Puig des Migdia (232 m).

▲ Torrent des Saluet

GR 221
STAGE 1

SECTION 1.2
50 mins

1

FROM COLL DES VENT TO PAS VERMELL

▲ Pine grove of Coll des Vent

On the Coll des Vent itself we come across two semi-detached lime kilns. The path forks. Our route will continue along a path, to the right in a NE direction, rather busy, that climbs a very steep crest. We go over a small pass —where we now get views of Cap de Llebeig and Sa Dragonera and behind us now Port d'Andratx and the coastline of Calvià— and we continue along the north face of a hill that extends until reaching Puig d'en Ric (312 m). The dominant pine forest has an undergrowth of garrigues with wild olive trees, reeds, European fan palm, white rockrose, heathers, mastic trees…, in which live spotted flycatchers, warblers, shrikes, as well as martens, rabbits and goats. In summer, the song of the cicadas is persistent.

With some almost flat sections and with not much gradient, the track reaches a vantage point, to the left of the tallest buildings in the Mont-port urbanisation, visible from the crest. Towards the north we see an elevation occupied by some communication antennas, which is the direction our path goes in.

In a few minutes we reach a hillock (258 m) after following the shade of the crag. A path, in a SE direction, links up with the Son Borràs urbanisation: we do not take this. In the opposite direction, NW, our path climbs the western side of Puig d'en Ric, and later on converges with a track that comes from Font Seca, one of the branches of Cala d'Egües watercourse, populated by small pine trees.

We climb along a good path in a N direction, go through an opening and reach a flat area where there is an old arcade, closed to the detour that enters the communication facilities, protected by a grille. From this point on, the path continues in a westerly direction and dies out close to the hill called Puntal Vermell (312 m). We should look carefully, because some 200 m from the antennas, we must leave the path and,

towards the right, following some boundary stones, climb to the crest. We will see without any difficulty the Pas Vermell (295 m). It is an imponderable vantage point over Sa Dragonera, the Sa Palomera valley and Sant Elm.

GR 221	SECTION 1.3
STAGE 1	45 mins

FROM PAS VERMELL TO SANT ELM

▲ Descent towards Sant Elm with Sa Dragonera in the background

The well-defined route follows, NE, a rough track marked by the reddish colour of the ferrous minerals. Sheltered by the crags we come across an old abandoned hut. Quickly descending and on an eroded route between reeds, small pine trees and European fan palms, the narrow path leaves the rough track and links up, at Coll de Sa Barrera (223 m), with a wider path, which covers the Tres Picons area. Notice a water tank to control the much-feared forest fires. On **Coll de Sa Barrera**, at the height of the water tank, we can see the scenery from a nearby vantage point.

From here begins a variant of some 9 km that allows us to reduce a stage of the GR. It has the inconvenience, however, of making us miss the charms of Sa Dragonera, the silence of the small valley of La Trapa and the first sea cliffs that form the Serra de Tramuntana. The variant begins at the Coll de Sa Barrera (223 m) along the cart track on the right, which in a NE direction comfortably drops towards the S'Arracó valley. Once in the village, first go

El Pas Vermell ▶

north towards Sa Clota, turn to the NW, and later climb the Camí de Ses Rotes de S'Hereu until it comes out again on our route, now within stage 2, close to Ses Basses.

If, from the abovementioned tank, we have decided to continue towards Sant Elm, we will go westwards; the track follows the crest closely, and close to a small panoramic view from a hillock, it forks. The right fork goes to a communication antenna on a hill (217 m) and the left towards the Canal d'en Sastre, closed and covered with pinewoods and garrigues. In summer, Eleonora's falcons provide the spectacle of their hunting and courting flights.

In a few minutes, at a crossing, our path is the one on the right, which drops steeply with older sections of path. At the next fork, we should continue on the right until we reach a plain with some buildings. We pass close to signs such as Sa Pineta. Shortly after, the path turns in a NW direction and, going downhill all the way, leads us to a pass (59 m) to the south of Puig Blanc (112 m). We follow the track on the right and at the first junction, after some 200 m, we turn left, to pass an asphalted path, before the Castell de Sant Elm (13th century), much restored, which was originally a hospital and oratory. It was owned by Archduke Louis Salvador and currently belongs to the Fundació Illes Balears. It cannot be visited. The left-hand path drops towards the Cala es Conills development, from where, by the first street on the right, we reach the beach of Sant Elm.

THE CASTLE OF SANT ELM

The restored Castell de Sant Elm, situated on a hill 63 m above the beach of En Gemec, is a building fortified in the 14th century and enlarged in the 16th century. It was initially designed as a hospital for sailors and oratory. In 1886 it was bought by Archduke Louis Salvador and is currently the property of the Fundació Illes Balears. It is a building of cultural interest but cannot, unfortunately, be visited. Built in 1302 by order of King Jaume II, it has been witness to many centuries of insecurity on these western coasts of Mallorca. From the castle, we link up with Carrer Cala es Conills which leads us to the small cove of the same name, suitable for bathing. There are usually some boats. A street links up with the beach of Sant Elm.

▲ Seahawk

▲ Castell de Sant Elm   ▼ Cala es Conills

SA DRAGONERA

Sa Dragonera, both from La Trapa and from the foot of its cliffs, is spectacularly beautiful. The northern cliffs, dark and with European fan palms and tall prickly pears, make us shudder. On the highest peak (343 m), the ruins of the old lighthouse of Na Pòpia remain silent between frequent fogs and the screams of gulls. The path climbs in tiring curves. One can reach the lighthouses on foot at the Llebeig and Tramuntana points from the houses of Cala Lledó, where the port and reception centre is. The islet is usually reached by boats that set sail from Sant Elm and Port d'Andratx. We must also consider its natural richness formed by a vegetation typical of the Mallorcan mountain coastline, subjected to extreme conditions of drought, sunshine and salinity, and for a very interesting fauna, especially for the abundance of endemic lizards (friendly and bold with human visitors) and for the presence of protected birds —osprey, European shag, Audouin's gull, Eleanora's falcon—, and migratory birds.

Sa Dragonera has an undeniable importance in the contemporary history of the Balearic Islands. It was the first natural space to be the subject of political controversy. Threatened by the construction of an urbanisation in the early 1970s, the island was invaded by surprise in July 1977 by an anarchist group, something that made the headlines in the Spanish and international press. Later on, and by means of long drawn out legal proceedings initiated and tenaciously sustained by the main local ecologist group (GOB), the island was declared non-developable (1987). Many demonstrations on the streets of Palma finally managed to defeat the intentions of the political groups in favour of the urbanisation, and, at the end of 1988, the island was acquired by the Consell de Mallorca and declared a natural park in 1995.

▲ **Island of Sa Dragonera**

▲ Sa Dragonera, from the La Trapa way   ▼ Lizard

GR 221 STAGE 1	SECTION 1.4 20 mins

FROM SANT ELM TO CAN TOMEVÍ

▲ **The corner of Sant Elm from the islet of Es Pantaleu**

From the beach of Cala en Gemec, we can take in the islet of **Es Pantaleu**, which is a refuge for many leisure boats. We walk on the pavement of the pedestrian street, Avinguda Jaume I, scattered with viewpoints. The street reaches a small square, Na Caragola. On the pavement area is the small harbour that serves as the jetty for the Na Margarita boat, which makes trips to Sa Dragonera. Going along Carrer de Cala en Basset we reach the northern district, S'Algar, an old fishermen's quarter. We cross the Plaça de Mossèn Sebastià Grau and continue the walk along the "avenue" of La Trapa, which soon becomes a rural path.

Some 900 m further on, after going along a watercourse shaded by the pine wood, we reach Can Tomeví, a small cultivated space dominated by a simple construction. Our route towards the old monastery of La Trapa begins just reside the entrance to Can Tomeví and goes —marked by signposts with the indication Cala en Basset— northwards, the same as the arrival. It is a spectacular short cut, which overcomes rough coastal crags.

GR 221 STAGE 1	SECTION 1.5
	50 mins

1

FROM CAN TOMEVÍ TO REFUGE OF LA TRAPA

▲ Balearic warbler (*Sylvia baleárica*)

Fortunately, despite frequent fires, this landscape facing us of **Es Freu de Sa Dragonera** has been preserved and forms such unforgettable places as the tower of **Cala en Basset** or the cove itself. As we climb upwards we will discover the simple beauty of this county. In the pine wood grows white rockrose, mastic trees and wild olive trees. We can observe blackbirds, spotted flycatchers, great tits, turtledoves, crossbills, and also some Balearic warblers (*Sylvia balearica*), a Balearic ornithological endemism, and gulls, among other species of interest. There is no lack of butterflies, wasps, bumblebees and bees. In a few minutes we will cross a cart track, which also comes from behind Can Tomeví, and we continue NE, climbing abandoned old terraces, occupied only by the pine trees now. We can see constructions relating to the activity of the colliers.

We arrive at the foot of the crag, leaving a less defined detour to the right. We are now overlooking the wood of Can Basset, Sa Dragonera, and what is called the Costa des Grecs, at the end of which appears Sant Elm.

With a very steep staggered climb, the narrow path goes through difficult terrain. A first panoramic pass reveals to

▲ Tower of Cala en Basset

us a perfect setting of Sa Dragonera and the defence tower of the cove. We cross the high part of the immediate watercourse and crown a second pass with even more extensive views. A flatter section takes us to the foot of the last pass, which we overcome along a providential terrace that turns away from the precipice and passes the rocky step. Below us is Cala en Basset, and we suddenly discover the **Vall de Sant Josep**, with its surprising collection of terraces, in the middle of which stands the old Trappist monastery.

A very clear path leads us to the main path to the monastery, which in turn takes us before the main façade of La Trapa.

▾ **La Trapa**

LA TRAPA

Situated in the Vall de Sant Josep, La Trapa has been, since 1980, the property of the Grup Balear d'Ornitologia i Defensa de la Natura (GOB), which bought it through public fundraising, with the participation of various nature protection societies and institutions. The Consell de Mallorca is responsible for its rehabilitation and running as a refuge on the *Ruta de Pedra en Sec*. The property measures 104 *quarterades*, approximately 315 acres.

The most important milestone in the history of this place is the founding of a Trappist monastery by a small community of monks who had taken refuge in Mallorca because of the French Revolution, after having been expelled from Normandy. Canon Pere Roig promoted the construction of some buildings (chapel, refectory, cells, workshops, storerooms, mill ...) in this valley, until then almost uninhabited, to accommodate the monks, dedicated to the Virgin Mary. In 1820 the religious orders were abolished and La Trapa abandoned. Time and pillaging condemned the place to oblivion and ruin, even when still surviving until today are the stones in the terrace building work, the architecture of the fountains and mines and the mill. Today, La Trapa invites one to remember the past and preserve the future. The viewpoint of Sa Dragonera over the gullies of Cala en Basset enable us to observe the flight of gulls, cormorants, peregrine falcons, Eleanora's falcons —between April and November they spend the winter in the Indian Ocean—, and cinereous shearwaters.

NATURE NOTES

Dwarf fan palm

1

Common crossbill

Male goat

TOWNS

PORT D'ANDRATX

This town, today eminently tourist-orientated, originated from a settlement of fishermen, who established themselves here in the 17th century. In the mid-19th century it took on importance as an export centre for the relatively important Andratx soap industry. The port area, a good natural shelter, has lost its popular charm and traditional calm to the benefit of the property, nautical and hotel industries. The results are clearly visible, since the residential constructions have invaded the sides around the port.

PRACTICAL GUIDE

Andratx Town Council
Av. de la Cúria, 1
07150 Andratx
Tel. +34 971 62 80 00
Transports Illes Balears (Tib)
Tel. +34 971 17 77 77
http://tib.caib.es
Tourist Information Office Port d'Andratx
Av. de Mateu Bosch
Edifici de la Llonja
Port d'Andratx
07157 Andratx
Tel. +34 971 67 13 00
Tourist and local information
www.andratx.net

Port d'Andratx has services of all kinds throughout the year. It is a first-class nautical tourist centre.

SANT ELM

The tourist centre of Sant Elm occupies the bay that is formed between Punta Blanca and Punta Galinda. Its origins probably date back to small agricultural and fishing settlements that occupied S'Algar and Cala Conills. It is thought that an old Roman way, the road from Sa Palomera to Palma, started right here. This area is notable in a special way for being the landing point of the Catalan expedition for the conquest of Mallorca under the command of King Jaume I, on the 7th of September 1229. The islet of Es Pantaleu was the first place this king set foot on land heard mass.

Sant Elm has several hotels and restaurants for all pockets, shops, chemist's, a chapel, a local information point, public transport and taxi service that links up with Andratx. The boat that crosses Es Freu to make the highly recommendable visit to the island of Sa Dragonera moors in the small port of Na Caragola.

PRACTICAL GUIDE

Andratx Town Council
Av. de la Cúria, 1
07150 Andratx
Tel. +34 971 62 80 00
Transports Illes Balears (Tib)
Tel. +34 971 17 77 77
http://tib.caib.es
Taxi Andratx
Tel. +34 971 13 63 98
Tourist Information Office of Sant Elm
Av. de Jaume I, 28- B
Sant Elm
07159 Andratx
Tel. +34 971 23 92 05
Tourist and local information
www.andratx.net

Sant Elm has a series of services (accommodation, restaurants, cafeterias, food shops, banks, chemists, medical attention), particularly during the high season (June to September). In winter, some of these services may be closed. It is basically a tourist resort, with very little life in winter.

GR 221 STAGE 2

Heights

900 m
800 m
700 m
600 m   **SECTION 2.1**
500 m
400 m
300 m
200 m
100 m — LA TRAPA
0 m

SES BASSES

SECTION 2.2

PLA DE
S'EVANGÉLICA

SECTION 2.3

COLL DE LA FONT
DES QUER

SECTION 2.4

REFUGI COMA
D'EN VIDAL

SECTION 2.5

ESTELLENCS

Distance: 20 km

Time: 6 h 35 mins

Difficulty: moderate

Maps:

Instituto Geográfico Nacional 1:25.000 – number 697-II

Editorial Alpina 1/25.000 Mallorca Tramuntana Sud

GR 221

6 h 35 mins Level of difficulty

🥾🥾🥾

2

STAGE
2

Departure
LA TRAPA
Arrival
ESTELLENCS

◄ **Way between reeds**   ▲ **Es Castellet and Puig de Galatzó**

New roads inexorably displace the old cart tracks, some medieval, that join Andratx with Estellencs. But the coastal areas of Ses Basses, Es Rajolí and S'Evangèlica enable us to cross landscapes full of solitude and magnificence. Here, nature and man seem to intensely grip the earth, always scant and poor, often dry. We leave behind us the Vall de Sant Josep and we will confront the rocky domain of Puig de S'Esclop, a geographical landmark that joins the municipal districts of Andratx, Estellencs and Calvià. At the time of writing, the Coma d'en Vidal refuge was not open. You should make sure you have accommodation booked in Estellencs.

N

0   0,5   1 km

Map | 41

2

GR 221 STAGE 2	SECTION 2.1 1 h

FROM LA TRAPA TO SES BASSES

▲ La Trapa

On leaving the refuge, a track winds its way across the Coll de Ses Ànimes (365 m) and reaches the adjoining valley of Sa Palomera, from where one can return to Sant Elm by the Can Tomeví path or turn at km 5 of the Ma-1030 road just by the Coll de Sa Palomera.

We will follow this track as far as the fifth bend to take a signposted path on the left, which passes between reeds and shrubs of gorse and furze, in the shadow of the white Puntals de La Trapa (454 m). We gradually climb up to a narrow stone pass that leads to the Es Forn estate, where there are some remains of cottages, terraces and coal silos.

The path worsens and bends to overcome the final slope. We come to a junction marked with a huge pile of stones. Towards the left, some 50 m away, is the **viewpoint of Morro d'En Fabioler**, at 450 m altitude. From the viewpoint, promoted by the veteran association Foment de Turisme de Mallorca (tourism promotion body), we can take in a new and exceptional image of Sa Dragonera and of the rocky coastal cliffs, vertical and hair-raising. At sunset, all our senses are insufficient to capture the telluric strength and impressive beauty of this spot.

From the junction marked by the pile of stones one can see Puig de Ses Basses, domain of goats marked by a geodesic crown on the head

The peak overlooks almost all the northern part of the district of Andratx and part of Calvià, as does, to the north and east, the coastline of Tramuntana overlooked by the imposing Puig de S'Esclop. Our route continues on a long downward path crossing the abrupt steps of the Marina de ses

Bardes until reaching a spot known as Ses Basses, where there are some cottages. Here, archaeologists have found remains of burials, fortifications and homes that speak of a long period of human occupation in prehistoric, Roman, Islamic and medieval times.

GR 221 STAGE 2	SECTION 2.2
	1 h 10 mins

FROM SES BASSES TO THE PLA DE S'EVANGÈLICA

▲ Ses Basses

The path turns into a track, takes two bends in descent, and leaves to the right the variant of the *Ruta de pedra en sec* that links up with S'Arracó via the Rotes de S'Hereu. Opposite stands out the pale craggy spot of Paret des Moro and the route of the path mentioned.

We, however, must continue along the main path, called Ses Basses. It stays at almost the same level until the bends allow us to overcome the Ses Pedrisses pass (395 m). The same cart track drops to the area of Es Campàs, where pine woods and cultivated fields coexist, beneath the silhouette of Puig des Campàs and Puig des Voltor. We will come across some buildings. Shortly before reaching the Ma-10 road, as it passes the **Coll de Sa Gremola**, we turn onto a path that we find on the left, dropping towards the Comellar de Sa Guixeria. A little further down, the path leaves the gully and, in a NE direction, links up with the track that climbs up to the Rajolí area. On the right and in no time at all, we will reach the Pla de S'Evangèlica, where the road passes.

Way from Ses Basses to Coll de Sa Gremola ▶

At the time of writing, the vegetation occupies the section of path that goes around the Comellar de Sa Guixeria and it is not at all easy to walk through. An alternative is not to go down to the Comellar de Sa Guixeria and continue along the Ses Basses path until the Coll de Sa Gremola (km 106) and follow the road towards the left, in the direction of Estellencs, for one kilometre, along which you also reach the Pla de S'Evangèlica. We advise prudence.

▲ Es Quer spring

GR 221 STAGE 2	SECTION 2.3 2 h 30 min

FROM PLA DE S'EVANGÈLICA TO THE COLL DE LA FONT DES QUER

Beside the road we cover the Pla de S'Evanglica as far as km 104.4, where there is a metalled road that climbs to the right, signposted as Coma des Cellers. We go through some properties with houses and go towards the high part of the previously mentioned coma (valley). The path climbs up the valley with a steep slope and several bends and dies out a bit further on, beside a high plateau of cultivated land and a cottage in ruins, Cas Carabinero. Behind this space, and in a NW direction, we follow an enclosed route that gains height until a pass in the rocky hill. The spot is known as **Es Pas Gran** (460 m). It has great views of the Pla de S'Evangèlica. In the distance one can make out the Morro d'en Fabioler.

Changing course, we now head NE, off-path, climbing the rocky spot cracked by erosion. We take a low sloping ridge that extends between the Coma des Cellers and that of Es Cucó Verd. The vegetation, impoverished by successive fires, is characterised by disperse pine trees, European fan palm, reeds and rockrose.

We cross the **Planes d'en Cabrit**, where the terrain is less steep, and suddenly we reach the Avenc d'en Trau and an adjacent fenced enclosure, with a *botador* (a type of stile).

The path becomes more defined and heads northwards. Almost flat, it goes over a pass and crosses the high part of the Comellar des Cucó Verd. After climbing a wall, we enter into the Ses Alquerioles estate, with lots of remains of stone landmarks and terraces.

We continue along the edges of the Ses Alquerioles plain. After passing a fence we come to a pass where a well appears to the left of the path. Heading north, we go along the base of a crag until reaching a crack that enables us to go over it. It is the **Pas d'en Ponça**.

With a steep slope, we drop down a long rocky ridge, along a route not yet signposted but marked with piles of stones. We reach a high plateau with piles of stones and borders, a demolished hut and a plot of land. It is quite a surprise to find these examples of agriculture in a spot that is currently so inhospitable. We are now 840 metres above sea level.

The route continues without a really clear definition. At this spot some piles of stones go towards the east, along a climb (optional) towards the Moleta de S'Esclop and the peak of the same name (928 m). From the peak, we can go down the western pass of the Puig that will take us to the Coll de la Font des Quer (737 m), situated between S'Esclop and Es Castellet (776 m), where we come into contact again with the main route.

▲ **El pas Gran**

This variant enables us to discover the **Caseta de n'Aragó**, the remains of which are a short distance from the peak, towards the south. It was built as a refuge for the astronomer, physicist and politician from Roussillon, Dominique François Aragó (1786-1853), who undertook studies measuring the meridian curve of the Earth. Aragó had arrived in Formentera and Mallorca in 1808. Here, his studies, which coincided with the war against Napoleon, were interpreted by the Mallorcan people as a form of spying. For this reason, he had to abandon his scientific tasks in S'Esclop.

▲ Cottage of N'Aragó   ▼ S'Esclop

2

If you do not take the option of climbing up to S'Esclop, we go round the north face of La Moleta. From the old ruined hut and plot we head off on a quick descent along the northeast side, between old terraces. The path, slow, faces east and descends as far as the area surrounding the Font des Quer, identifiable by the closeness of a black poplar beside an isolated crag. The spring is usually dry.

From the spring, a bridal path drops eastwards and leads us to the next mountain pass (737 m), closed to the left by Es Castellet, also called Penya Blanca.

GR 221 STAGE 2	SECTION 2.4
	40 mins

FROM COLL DE LA FONT DES QUER TO SA COMA D'EN VIDAL

▲ Sunset

On our right comes the path that drops from the peak of S'Esclop. The path goes eastwards and passes close to another plot of land. On the right we see the ruins of Sa Caseta de S'Esclop. We start a gentle drop that leads us in a short time to a wall that marks the boundary of the Estellencs district. From this point, a variant in a northeast direction, not very well defined, links up with the climb to Galatzó which comes from La Boal de Ses Serveres. We jump over a wall and, in the west, we find ourselves in the Coma d'en Vidal. Suddenly, the valley and the path, now wider, turn north through a difficult pine wood with common juniper, reed and mastic tree covering the ground except for the escarped rocky spots of the Serra des Pinotells, to our right.

The ruins of the Font des Moro mark the entrance to the cultivated land that surrounds the **Coma d'en Vidal refuge**. The estate (50 ha) has been public since 2002. At the time of writing, the refuge was still not yet open to the public.

▲ Rocky spots of Sa Coma

GR 221 STAGE 2	SECTION 2.5 1 h 15 mins

FROM SA COMA D'EN VIDAL TO ESTELLENCS

▲ Coma d'en Vidal refuge

We continue heading NE on the path that links the refuge with the Ma-10 road. The route is initially flat and is in good condition, and runs between the cultivated land of Sa Coma. We pass two consecutive openings. On our left runs the stream called Torrent des Gorgs. The track starts to drop with a steep slope and continuous bends. As we go down, the crests of the Serra des Pinotells, on our right, become increasingly spectacular and we discover new panoramic views of the coast.

After 35 minutes descent, we reach a beautiful space shaded by large holm-oaks where there is a water tank for fighting forest fires. Very nearby, we will leave a path that, to the right, goes to **Sa Boal de Ses Serveres**. It is a space adapted as a recreational area, bordered by two large rocky spots, Morro des Pinotells and Morro de Ses Serveres.

To the left, on a steep and fast route, the path drops to the Ma-10 road from Andratx to Estellencs (km 97). After the fourth bend, and now within sight of the road, we turn to the right along a path that comes out at km 96.7. We cross it and, going down along the embankment of the road, we continue along a wide path that enters into the pine wood (towards the left). Just after a curve to the right, we come out on the Camí Vell (old way) from Andratx to Estellencs. On the right, this old path climbs and joins the road at the Coll des Pi, where there is a petrol station. We go along a bit of the Ma-10 and shortly after the Coll des Pi, to the left and at kilometre 95.6, we take the old road again. After four steep bends downhill, the way levels out a little for an easier arrival in Estellencs.

While we approach the first houses of the town, we pass on the left the local cemetery and the turning for the cove. Then, Carrer Eusebi Pascual, to the right, will lead us once again to the Ma-10 road, now inside the town.

PUIG DE GALATZÓ

If we want to know more about the county, we recommend the optional climb to Puig de Galatzó (1,027 m), in the shape of a pyramid and isolated from the other high peaks of the Serra de Tramuntana. On clear days, you can see the immediate way ahead of the Ruta de Pedra en Sec, as if it were a model.

It is a climb of medium-hard difficulty, suitably signposted. It leaves from Sa Boal de Ses Serveres and marks out the climb to Galatzó via the Pas des Cossi and the Pas de na Sabatera. It takes a little under 2 hours to reach the top. The variant back down goes through the wood of Son Fortuny by Sa Boal de ses Fonts and the Pas de Sa Copa d'Or, to return to Sa Boal de Ses Serveres. The trip back takes 1 h 30 mins.

In the public estate of Son Fortuny there are some interesting routes to be done.

▲ Morro des Pinotells

▼ Puig de Galatzó

NATURE NOTES

Blackberry

Rosemary

Holm-oak

TOWNS

THE TOWN OF ESTELLENCS AND LA CALA

Estellencs is a place name with an old and uncertain origin. It appears documented as *Stellenchs* in 1234. Some scholars believe that is has Arab origins, while others think it is Germanic. The town is a typical heaping-up of houses between steep and narrow streets. In the lovely centre of Estellencs stands, reformed, the church dedicated to Saint John the Baptist. The church still seems to seek protection from the old defence tower attached (16th century). There is a second square-shaped tower, the En Tem Alemany, which perhaps also misses the thrill of the dangers that came from the sea in another time. The streets in the low part of the town conserve corners where the traditional architecture has remained almost unaltered, with the occasional oil press. The town is connected to the coast along Carrer de los Magraners, which links up with an asphalted path that goes down to La Cala, the small harbour where boats shelter. Towards the north appear the escarped edges of the Estellencs coastline. The higher part of the town, S'Arraval, has a layout of terraced streets and provides the best panoramic views of the setting.

PRACTICAL GUIDE

Estellencs Town Council
Carrer de sa Síquia, 4
07192 Estellencs
Tel. +34 971 61 85 21
ajuntament@ajestellencs.net
Transports Illes Balears (Tib)
Tel. +34 971 17 77 77
http://tib.caib.es
Tourist and local information
www.ajestellencs.net

The Estellencs district has services of all kinds. In winter, though, some of these services may not be available. You should be aware that it is a small district with little activity in winter.

2

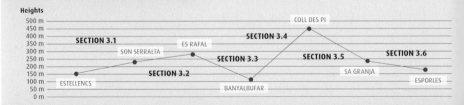

GR 221 STAGE 3

Heights

- 500 m
- 450 m — COLL DES PI
- 400 m
- 350 m — SECTION 3.1 — SECTION 3.4
- 300 m — ES RAFAL
- 250 m — SON SERRALTA
- 200 m — SECTION 3.3 — SECTION 3.5 — SECTION 3.6
- 150 m — SECTION 3.2 — SA GRANJA
- 100 m — ESTELLENCS — ESPORLES
- 50 m — BANYALBUFAR
- 0 m

Distance: 15 km

Time: 5 h 15 min.

Difficulty: moderate

Maps:

Instituto Geográfico Nacional 1:25.000 – number 697-II y 670-III

Editorial Alpina 1:25.000 Mallorca Tramuntana Sud

GR 221

5 h 15 mins

Level of difficulty

🥾🥾🥾

3

STAGE

3

Departure

ESTELLENCS

Arrival

ESPORLES

‹ Esporles   ▲ Cala d'Estellencs

The stage, gentle and with panoramic views, goes along an old royal route that joined Estellencs and Esporles, before the construction of the current asphalted roads. With gentle slopes, it uses sections of paved and terraced bridle paths, and visits properties and stately homes of the big properties of the traditional nobility —such as Son Serralta, Planícia, Es Rafal and Es Collet—, pillars of the history and economy of the area. A certain, undefined Mediterranean calm connects Estellencs, Banyalbufar and Esporles more with the past than with the present which almost strangles the island. It is a good idea to book accommodation in Esporles.

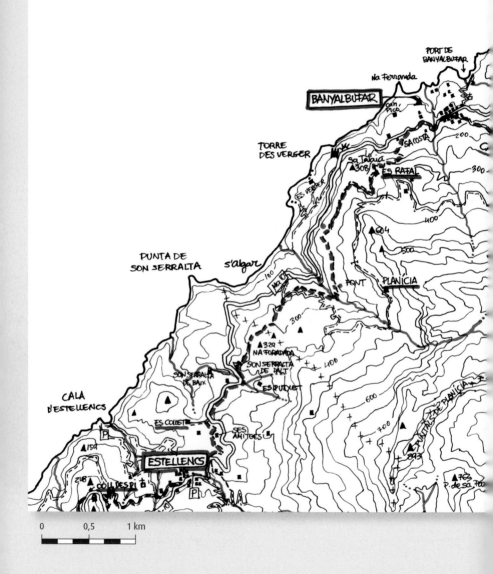

PORT DE
BANYALBUFAR

Na Ferranda

BANYALBUFAR

Can Pico

SA COSTA

TORRE
DES VERGER

ES VERGER

Sa Talaia
▲308

ES RAFAL

▲604

PUNTA DE
SON SERRALTA

s'algar

NA LUT

FONT

PLANICIA

NA FORADADA
▲329

SON SERRALTA
DE DALT

SON SERRALTA
DE BAIX

ES PUIXET

CALA
D'ESTELLENCS

ES COLLET

SES
AMITGES

ESTELLENCS

PUIG DE PLANICIA

▲893

▲150

▲248

COLL DES PI

P

P

▲763
P. de sa Pou

0   0,5   1 km

Map | 61

3

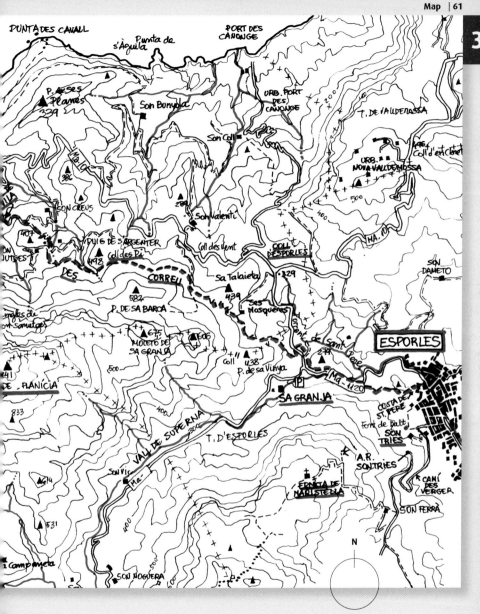

PUNTA DES CAVALL

PORT DES CANONGE

Punta de s'Àguila

P. DE SES PLANES 339

Son Bunyola

URB. PORT DES CANONGE

T. DE VALLDEMOSSA

380

Son Coll

URB. NOVA VALLDEMOSSA

Coll d'en Claret

MA-10

SON CREUS

289

Son Valentí

500

407

PUIG DE S'ARGENTER 498

Coll des Pi

Coll des Vent

COLL D'ESPORLES

329

MA-10

SON DAMETO

DES

CORREU

Sa Talaieta

439

SON JUTGES

587

P. DE SA BARCA

Ses Mosqueres

ESPORLES

angles de on somuiges

675

606

MOLETO DE SA GRANJA

Coll 438

P. de sa Vinya

Torrent de Sant Pere

274

41

DE PLANÍCIA

500

MA-1120

SA GRANJA

COSTA DE ST. PERE

833

400

VALL DE SUPERNA

200

T. D'ESPORLES

Font de Dalt

SON TRIES

A.R. SON TRIES

CAMÍ DES VERGER

614

SON VIC

MA-

ERMITA DE MARISTEL·LA

531

SON FERRÀ

i Campaneta

SON NOGUERA

N

GR 221 STAGE 3	**SECTION 3.1** 30 mins

FROM ESTELLENCS TO SON SERRALTA

▲ Es Collet

The main street or Sa Síquia (Ma-10 road), in the direction of Banyalbufar, leads to the old washhouse, near to the bridge over the steam. At km 93.90 on the left of the road we come across the **real path from Estellencs to Banyalbufar**. After an initial steep descent, it climbs in the same direction and among farmland, until connecting after some 15 minutes with the entrance path to the Es Collet property. Take a look back to admire once again the haughty profile of Puig de Galatzó. Es Collet conserves its proud architecture, crowned by the defence tower that guarded over this strategic spot.

We take the road and walk along with care for some 600 metres. At km 92.15 we cross it to take a cemented and steep cart track that will lead us to the façades of the houses of Son Serralta de Dalt.

The coastline views extend as far as the Morro d'en Fabioler.

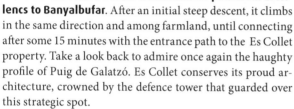

GR 221 STAGE 3	**SECTION 3.2** 1 h 30 mins

FROM SON SERRALTA TO ES RAFAL

The GR turns towards the back of the large house and continues northwards, rising gently and on a cart track. After about 100 metres, in front of a fenced opening, the route turns to

the left and becomes a path that runs through a shady and pleasant wood. An old stone opening leads into the holm-oak wood. The bridle path we follow is well defined all the way. Close to the sea appears the corner of S'Algar, with a small reef close to the Punta de Son Serralta and the Torreta des Verger. We are now within the district of Banyalbufar.

Follow a climb towards a pass, with splendid views towards the Planícia valley, with the property sheltered at the foot of the crags of the hill with the same name.

We go down a well-signposted section of the GR beside a dry stone wall. We cross a gully and reach an asphalted path that links **Planícia** with the road. At the time of writing, a legal ruling prohibited passing through the Es Rafal estate. Therefore, at this point of the GR, we should go left and go down to the Ma-10 road. Then, and with great care, walk the 3 km to Banyalbufar.

If circumstances change and the right to pass is won back, we could cross the Planícia path and continue in the same direction as the walk. A short climb leads to an equally flat section that crosses the Bosc de na Vergunya, a big attraction. The paved path drops a little, as far as an opening and a gully, which we cross to climb up the other side. Making several zigzags we pass through terraced land of old crops.

We link up with a main cart track, close to the Font de S'Obi, generally dry, close to an old dead pine tree and a hut. We continue along this path to the left (N), with a slight slope, between terraces and olive trees, reeds and small pine. To the west we can make out the hill of Es Grau and the Morro d'en Fabioler.

We reach an iron gate that we must cross. The track turns into a path. We

◄ ▲ **Elements of dry masonry**

keep on in the same direction and at the same level, leaving a turning to our right. Shortly after, the path once again reverts to a cart track and passes by another olive grove.

Along the Ruta de Pedra en Sec, and having left a little further ahead a path that comes from the Font des Garbell, we reach a pass that coincides with a junction. We continue along the left-hand path, paved and downhill, until reaching a new plot of land, with views of the nearby houses of Es Rafal and, in the background, of the Serra range: Punta de Sóller, Sa Foradada, Puig Major, Es Teix…

GR 221 STAGE 3	SECTION 3.3 20 mins

FROM RAFAL TO BANYALBUFAR

We reach Es Rafal, which dates from the 14th century and has a distinguished and simple façade with remains of fortification. From the large plot situated at the end of the north façade of Es Rafal we begin the downhill part along a magnificent bridle path. We cross a wall by an opening with metallic gate and continue down through the shaded wood, a mosaic of vegetation and winged life: great tits, robins, warblers, blackbirds and turtledoves.

▲ Vine

Very shortly we once again enter a humanised space. The stone terraces, cottages, irrigation ditches and washhouses indicate its use of intensive farming (vines, vegetables and fruit). The whole complex is crossed by our way, called the **Camí de Sa Costa**. The last section, uneven and rectilinear, reaches the Ma-10 road, right by the entrance to Banyalbufar.

CAMÍ DES CORREU

This is the name of the old royal way, dating from 1401, connecting Banyalbufar and Esporles and coinciding with our GR. It is not clear if its name, *correu* or post, corresponds to its use for sending letters, or simply a general name of transporting travellers by track. The final section of the track also joined Sa Granja (an old Cistercian monastery) with the island's capital, the city of Palma. It is a comfortable route, without any steep gradients and with lovely views.

▲ Black-headed warbler (*Sylvia melanocephala*)

▲ Camí des Correu

▼ Banyalbufar

GR 221 STAGE 3	SECTION 3.4
	1 h

FROM BANYALBUFAR TO COLL DES PI

▲ Square Town

We set off from the town square, with our backs to the church façade, and we walk up the asphalted and narrow Car- rer Jeroni Alberti. We pass some old buildings such as Cas Batle Negre and Son Borguny (now a tourist establishment). On the outskirts, the path takes the name of Camí de la Font de la Vila. On our right is the large gardened house of Son Vives. The GR sign an- nounces: "Esporles 2 h 30 mins". After some 300 metres we see, on the right, a large washhouse. As we will see throughout the

▲ Banyalbufar

climb up, farming on terraces depended on a good irrigation system, made up of a series of watercouses and canals.

The route, heading southeast and with a steep gradient, provides us with views of the terraced spaces towards Cala de Banyalbufar, Coll de Sa Bastida and the high point of Ses Planes (339 m). Further over to the right is Coll des Pi, which our route passes by. And now we see, further to the right, the rocky spots of the Mola de Planícia (941 m).

Twenty minutes after leaving the village, the way levels out and narrows, populated by large holm-oaks and nourished by the Torrent d'en Roig stream. Above the way is the source of the **Font de la Vila**, which supplies water to the whole county. From here lead two main canals, the Dalt and Baix irrigation channels.

▲ The marina of Banyalbufar

▲ Steep banks alongside the sea   ▼ The large washhouse of Son Vives

The cart track describes a series of bends and connects farms and plots. The natural vegetation of pines, strawberry trees, reeds and myrtles mix with farmed areas and olive groves.

Some 20 minutes after the source we come to the Camí de Sa Font des Garbell, which we must cross. On the right we have left behind the Son Sanutges cement works. We have to continue straight on, between borders, heading south and with a steep gradient. Shortly after, the way changes direction towards the east and passes through a wooded and shady area. We cross over a wall where a new sign appears: "Esporles 1 h 40 mins / Banyalbufar 40 mins".

In a short distance we go over another stone wall. The way, almost level, goes through the holm-oak wood, in the direction of the Coll des Pi with a final straight section of magnificent paving. On our left we can make out Puig de S'Argenter, which takes its name from an old silver mine

▼ Coll des Pi

GR 221 STAGE 3	SECTION 3.5 1 h 30 mins

FROM COLL DES PI TO PLA DES MURTAR AND SA GRANJA

In 5 minutes, we reach a small viewpoint that looks out over the coastline of Valldemossa and Sóller, as well as the heights of Es Teix. We walk a long, flat section, marked by the odd limekiln. At a crossroads, we discover a panoramic plain known popularly as S'Era des Moro. It was used to dry holm-oak bark to be used in the textile industries. Alongside the sea we can make out the country estate and large house of Son Bunyola and the coast of Port des Canonge. Further north is **Sa Foradada.**

Shortly after the piece of land, the descent begins. After a watercourse, we climb a pass enclosed by a wall. The sign reminds us: "Esporles 40 mins". This is the Coll de Sa Talaieta (439 m), a place known also as **La Potada des Cavall**, due to the imprint of a legendary horse's hoof in the paved surface. The path follows half a dozen bends and a new well-paved section. We continue through the wood, in a gentle descent.

After another limekiln, the gradient increases. An opening with a gate marks the point where we leave the wood behind and enter into an olive grove. Staggered and winding, the path reaches the Pla de ses Mosqueres, with a plantation of olive trees. We go through another opening with a small gate that offers views of the mountainous profiles of La Mola de Son Pacs. A few minutes from the gate, the path suddenly turns towards the left and immediately reaches the road close to Pla des Murtar, which we cross. The sign says "Esporles 30 mins / Banyalbufar 2 h". Two minutes walk on the left side of the road takes us to the view of the houses of Sa Granja.

▲ Sa Granja

**GR 221
STAGE 3**

SECTION 3.6

25 mins

3

FROM PLA DES MURTAR TO ESPORLES

▲ **Close to Sa Granja**

Sa Granja is a country estate that still conserves the splendid architecture of its golden age. Today it is open as an ethnologic museum with a very local atmosphere and a restaurant. It features the beautiful "loggia" that contrasts with the solid construction of a traditional air and the historical gardens. Its origins go way back in time, since it was a Cistercian monastery, built by the Catalan conquistadors over a Muslim farmstead.

The richness of Sa Granja is based in part on its springs. Alongside our route runs the water of the Font Major to Esporles. In the past there had been several mills and hydraulic turbines in the area.

We discover, towards the west, the Vall de Superna, set between the wooded heights of Sa Fita del Ram and La Mola de Planícia. At the end, the Puig de Galatos watches over.

The GR converges with the road, goes over the Torrent de Sant Pere and continues on the other side. The setting, shady, has banana trees, ashes, elms and black poplars. From here the path is called Sant Pere. The signpost says "Esporles 15 mins".

We climb between borders for a few minutes, until a plain provides us with the landscape of the mountains that surround Esporles. Towards the NE we can recognise the rocks of La Mola de Son Pacs or Son Ferrandell, where the next stage crosses. The **Costa de Sant Pere**, staggered and finally asphalted, leads us alongside the parish church, dedicated to Saint Peter. We are in the centre of this mountain village.

**NATURE
NOTES**

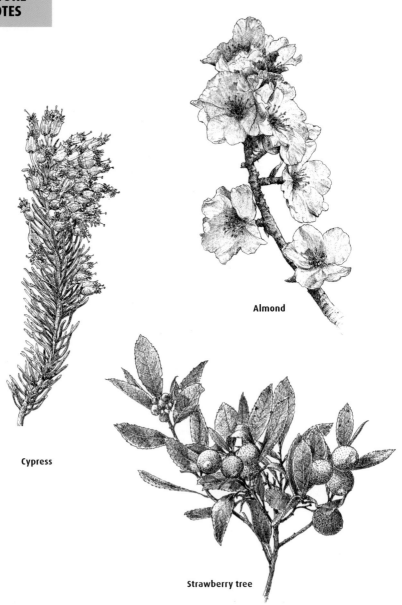

Almond

Cypress

Strawberry tree

3

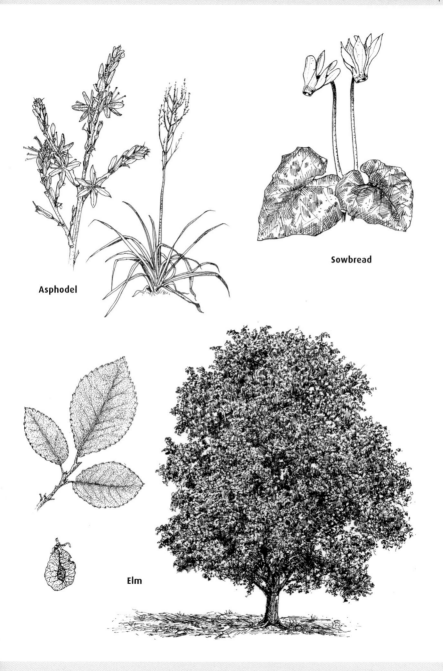

Asphodel

Sowbread

Elm

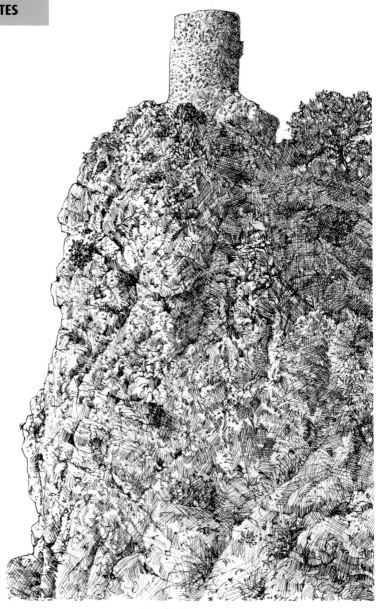

Torre des Verger

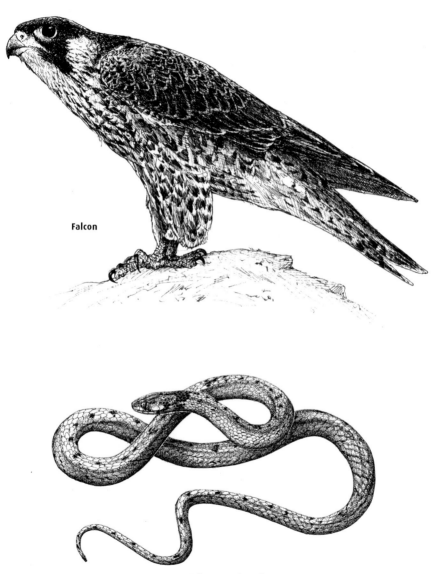

Falcon

False smooth snake

TOWNS

BANYALBUFAR

Mountain and seafaring town, Banyalbufar historically belonged to Esporles until its administrative segregation in the 19th century. The name comes from Islamic roots with a meaning equivalent to construction "at sea level". It was ruled by the landowners who held power in La Baronia, an administrative area encumbered to the Kings of Aragon. The large house of La Baronia, with courtyard and defensive tower, stands to the left of the road in the shade of the parish church of La Nativitat. The large house was once the vicarage and is today a hotel. Via Carrer Es Penyal we can visit the high district of the town. If we go down Carrer Es Pont and continue along the Camí des Molí we reach the area of Es Cós after crossing the orchards in borders that characterise the outskirts of the town. Banyalbufar prospered in the last century due to the production of tomatoes on the branch, sold all over the island and exported to Barcelona. Today the cultivation of another highly appreciated product has been recovered: Malvasia grapes for wine. Es Cós, where there is a car park, is a rocky platform that provides a great view of the marine and the adjoining port. A low terrace drops to the rocky place, close to some water mills of Islamic origin, built on the cliff, and used to grind the grain. In the cove there is a small boat harbour and a swimming area.

PRACTICAL GUIDE

Banyalbufar Town Council
Plaça de la Vila, 2
07191 Banyalbufar
Tel. +34 971 14 85 80
Transports Illes Balears (Tib)
Tel. +34 971 17 77 77
http://tib.caib.es
Tourist and local information
www.ajbanyalbufar.net

The town of Banyalbufar has all kinds of services. In winter, some of these services may not be available. You should realise that it is a small town, with little activity in winter.

ESPORLES

Where we arrive, the Plaça de Espanya, is where the Passeig del Rei begins, the town's main street and passes the road to Banyalbufar and Estellencs and to Palma. Esporles has fine examples of popular architecture. The centres of Sa Vila Nova and Es Rafal have houses that conserve the appearance of the past three centuries, with the peculiar Arab tiling or paintings and the terraced stone streets. The parish church —dating from 1904— replaced a much older place of worship. It has a beautiful altarpiece in the high altar, a jewel from the 17th century, dedicated to Saint Peter, patron saint of the town. Sa Vila Vella is the district occupying the left bank of the Torrent de Sant Pere, which crosses the town. Esporles has shops of all kinds, restaurants, cafeterias, bakers, chemist's, banks, etc.

PRACTICAL GUIDE

Esporles Town Council
Plaça d'Espanya, 1
07190 Esporles
Tel. +34 971 61 00 02
ajuntament@ajesporles.net
Transports Illes Balears (Tib)
Tel. +34 971 17 77 77
http://tib.caib.es
Tourist and local information
www.ajesporles.net

Esporles has all kinds of services. It is a very lively town and close to Palma. The council web page provides information about accommodation.

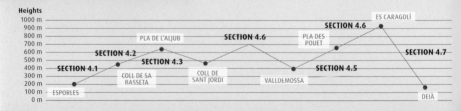

Heights

ES CARAGOLÍ

SECTION 4.6

PLA DE L'ALJUB

SECTION 4.6

PLA DES POUET

SECTION 4.2

SECTION 4.3

SECTION 4.7

SECTION 4.1

COLL DE SA BASSETA

COLL DE SANT JORDI

VALLDEMOSSA

SECTION 4.5

ESPORLES

DEIÀ

Distance: 19 km

Time: 6 h 50 mins

Difficulty: very difficult

Maps:

Instituto Geográfico Nacional 1/25.000 - numbers 670-III and 670-IV

Editorial Alpina 1/25.000 Mallorca Tramuntana South and Tramuntana Central

GR 221

6 h 15 mins Level of difficulty

4

STAGE 4

Departure
ESPORLES
Arrival
CAN BOI REFUGE

◄ Sa Beurada spring   ▲ Son Ferrandell plain

La Mola de Son Pacs is abrupt and uninhabited. It provides a surprising diversity of environments: limestone rocky hills, deep watercourses, woods and rocky spots, fissures... In the past it provided raw materials and work for a relatively numerous population. This is borne out by the ethnological trace left behind by road labourers, coal miners, lime workers, shepherds, hunters, lumberjacks... Today it conserves an interesting forest ecosystem. The large country estates that surround La Mola y and the mountain in the Valldemossa area are placed over the prints left by prehistoric and Islamic times. Valldemossa and Deià are delightful villages that really must be visited. Illustrious figures have linked their names with them for eternity: Chopin and Aurore Dupin (George Sand) in Valldemossa; Robert Graves in Deià. Archduke Louis Salvador of Austria, relative of the known Sissi, bought up many estates on this part of the coast.

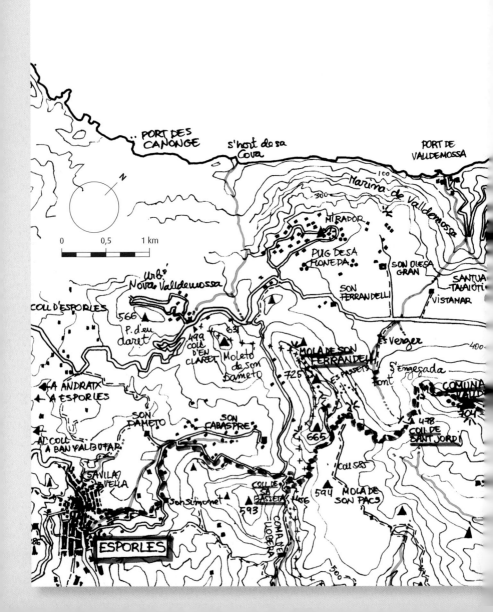

Map | 83

4

GR 221 STAGE 4 — SECTION 4.1 — 1 h

FROM ESPORLES TO COLL DE SA BASSETA

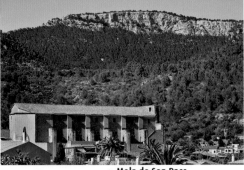
▲ Mola de Son Pacs

On our way towards the valley of Son Ferrandell, we walk along the singular district of Vila Vella in Esporles. We leave from the Plaça de Espanya, with the façade of the church behind us, and walk along Carrer Nou de Sant Pere. Over a small bridge we cross the stream and the junction with Carrer Major and Carrer Sa Creu, and in a few minutes we reach the Placeta des Pla. If we look back we will discover a beautiful view of the town, with the traditional architecture of stately buildings and those of a more simple style, surrounded by gardens and some orchards. In the background one can see the parish and the mountain of **Fita del Ram**, where the small hermitage of Maristel·la and the monument dedicated to the Heart of Jesus stand out, an excellent viewpoint.

From the small square, with a humble fountain, we continue on the right along Carrer Mateu Font, heading east. At the junction we see the sign "Son Cabaspre", which leads us to a turning to the right. We cross the stream of the same name over a bridge and alongside the stream, on the left, we climb up via an asphalted path, shaded by reedbed, banana tree, wild olive trees and holm-oaks. The path, which heads northwards, passes among terraced orchards. The valley gradually opens out and provides new landscapes. The immediate environment is made up of wooded hills or with olive and almond trees.

The narrow way turns towards the left and crosses the stream (small bridge). Straight ahead, take a steep cart track that follows the course of the stream. From an adjoining bend we can take in the good views of the valley we have left behind. Further on we can see the spurs of Es Verger and Es Pouet de Sobremunt, to the west, La Mola de Planícia with Es Puntals and, facing the route ahead, El Penyal des Migdia, the spur of La Moleta de Son Cabaspre.

4

We come out on the asphalted track of Son Cabaspre, which we must follow to our left (W) to the entrance of gateway to the rural urbanisation of **Son Cabaspre**. Opposite we see the limits of the Vall de Superna, Lla Mola de Planícia and Puig de Galatzó, with its characteristic pyramidal profile.

Ignoring diverse turnings from the path to the left, we reach an entrance crowned by beams which indicates the arrival at

▾ Esporles

the urbanisation. Opposite, on our path, we can see the south face of La Mola de Son Cabaspre, with its wide strip of cliffs, copper-coloured or pale according to the light of day.

In this setting there are some country estates: Son Dameto, a beautiful property already documented in 1653, which occupies a privileged space overlooking the high valleys of Esporles; **Son Simonet**, dates from the 17th century, much reformed, with a garden adorned with tall palm trees; Son Cabaspre, positioned at the end of the small valley. The houses usually had a wine cellar, chapel and oil mill, and some even had a large library. Their economy was based on the cultivation of olives and forestry, some crops and livestock.

Our route, from the entrance gate, turns along the first way, asphalted, —on the way to Sa Font des Bosc—, which we find on our right, towards the northeast, and climbing. The road winds its way along the northwest side of Moleta de Son Cabaspre (595 m), a spectacular rocky spot. Among the terraces, we approach the wood, the Font des Joncs springs from a mine. Shortly after passing the turning called the Sa Vall de ses Mules

▲ Strawberry trees

path, going upwards, a path closed off by a gate appears on the right (signposted as the Sa Coma Llobera path). After walking some 200 m we reach the Coll de Sa Basseta (457 m), where there is a concrete pond and drinking trough. This is the meeting place between the line of the central crest of La Mola de Son Pacs and La Moleta de Son Cabaspre, a suitable spot for having a bite to eat and recovering one's strength.

The valley of Son Cabaspre from Sa Mola ▶

▲ The marine of Valldemossa

We will see a path that begins at the pass and climbs in a northerly direction. We immediately take a path that turns to the right and rises steeply, zigzagging towards the side of an elongated rocky spot. We reach a small pass where we find the remains of a coalmining spot, very frequent all over this wood. We continue in the same direction and pass alongside some thrush hunting spots, to reach the foot of a boundary wall, which we must go over.

The wall marks the boundary between the municipalities of Esporles and Valldemossa, where we have already walked. To the west, following the line of the wall, we reach the edge of the cliffs to take in a splendid view across the county of Esporles and the coastline of de Banyalbu-

▲ Puig de sa Moneda

▲ Water tank   ▼ Oven

far. Facing northeast, we drop down through the holm-oak wood until coming across a new silo and hut.

We immediately climb up winding our way alongside a dry masonry wall. In ten minutes, we reach a cart track, which we follow in a northerly direction until reaching a high plateau where it forks off. We must take the left fork, rising gently and stony, within the holm-oak wood, heading north-northwest. We pass a turning to our left and another to our right and in five minutes we are before another junction. Beside us there are some silos and huts.

We take the cart track on the left. We immediately reach a flat piece of land, at 615 m altitude, where we come across the vaulted hut and a tank/deposit that was inhabited by colliers, lumberjacks and swineherds until a couple of generations ago. It shows an example of mountain exploitation, frequent in many places in the Mallorcan mountain range. We continue in a northwest direction, along a path that climbs an open watercourse, with new collieries. We pass close to a large fissure, leave a turning on the left, and after some bends, another turning to the right in the form of a descending path. To the west, off the path and following some piles of stones, one can see the highest part of **La Mola de Son Pacs** (726 m), a place known as Puntals or Mola de Son Ferrandell.

▲ **Sa Mola wood**

GR 221 STAGE 4

SECTION 4.3
40 mins

FROM PLA DE L'ALJUB TO COLL DE SANT JORDI

▲ Vistamar

Continuing the route from Pla d'Aljub, we go back to the piece of flat land with the tank (615 m). At the crossroads we follow the left-hand way and the abovementioned crossroads. On arrival, we now take the left-hand path, heading north, until coming up to a wall built alongside the rocky points. Towards the east, without losing sight of the wall, the path reaches two silos and forks off. The left fork is packed in by an uneven pass with a low wall and with a staggered slope. Between the wall and a mailing we drop steeply until reaching the Coll de Sant Jordi, where there is an opening with an iron gate.

GR 221 TAGE 4

SECTION 4.4
1 h 10 mins

FROM COLL DE SANT JORDI TO VALLDEMOSSA

▲ Downward step of Sa Mola

To our right extends the wood of Sa Baduia, at the head of glacial valley. We cross the opening and we see, to the north, the steep bends of the climb up to **Comuna de Valldemossa**, along a well-defined path, in the wood. We very shortly get a good view of the north face of La Mola de Son Pacs, with clear colours, in contrast to the rocky parts of its western face. Our path reaches the crest of Sa Comú. The climb, really quite tough, involves ascending the side of S'Engegada, almost 220 m difference in height.

We pass alongside a stone hut, square in shape and with an improvised uralite roof, and further on, beside one of the many *colls de tords* (narrow passes between trees or rocks where thrushes pass through and where traps are set to catch them).

The hunter, seated with his back to the narrow pass, prepares a wire net opened by means of two long reeds. When the thrush comes, the hunter traps it with a skilful movement of the reeds. This traditional technique has very old roots and many hunters on the Serra use it.

On the left appears the treeless rocky space, with an altitude of approximately 700m. Passing another hut, we cross a wall and then a rocky mountainside, where the path becomes unclear. To the left is the crest of the peak (709 m). In the same direction as we are walking we pass a turning to the right and reach a pass between a rocky spot. On the right is the platform of another *coll de tord* that serves as a wonderful watch tower to overlook the county of S'Estret de

▲ **Ses Mossetes**

Valldemossa, surrounded by the foothills of La Mola de Son Pacs and Na Fàtima, as well as a large part of the islands plain. We follow, going down gently, a narrow crest, with views of both sides of the path, now more defined. We reach a coal silo, alongside an arcade.

From the silo and in the same direction, we continue the descent along a narrow watercourse (Ses Mossetes), between crags, where the path winds its way down. In a couple of minutes a square pond appears where the path forks, although the two narrow paths come together further down, in the place called En Penyalot. We will take the right-hand fork, until reaching a wall with slate steps. Passing the wall, at an intersection, we take the path on the left that passes a hut and quickly

▲ The water tank of En Penyalot

drops down to another wall. Suddenly it goes towards a tank with vaulting that overlooks a small plain. Beside it stands a roofless arcade, attached to a rocky support, **En Penyalot**, an old dwelling of the colliers, swineherds and lumberjacks who worked in Sa Comuna.

From En Penyalot, we follow the signs, towards the north; in a quick descent we reach an opening, which we go through. The winding path moves closer to the right of a dividing wall, with steps and stony in sections. Shortly before the following opening we will see a cross carved out of a crag. In a few moments we come to the Font de na Llambies, which springs from the bottom of a vaulted mine, with a dry masonry wall. The spring supplied the water to the monastery of Sa Cartoixa from 1656.

We cross a small iron gate and continue on the left of the houses of Sa Teulera in a row protected by a wall. If we continue we will reach the opening that leads to the house, and the wide path that comes from the town of Valldemossa. If we want to visit the **Molí de Sa Beata**, here we will come across a turning to the left that will lead us to the hill (469 m) where we will find the famous mill as well as an oratory with a small altar and altarpiece dedicated to the Immaculate Conception, escorted by Saint Catalina Thomas and the Blessed Ramon Llull, and the flour mill of the Carthusians (18th century)

The path from Sa Teulera to the town borders the hill and after passing below the aqueduct (which brings the water from Na Llambies to the Carthusian monastery) it reaches the Son Mossènyer mill, with Arabised elements. This large country house, today restored and headquarters of the Jorge Luís Borges Foundation, was owned by the Carthusians from the mid-17th century. The concrete path ends in front of the entrance to the gardens of Sa Cartoixa, at the beginning of Carrer Uruguay. This entrance to Valldemossa will soon be altered.

GR 221 STAGE 4	SECTION 4.5 45 mins

FROM VALLDEMOSSA TO PLA DES POUET

▲ Finch

We leave the historic centre of **La Cartoixa** behind us and cross the road or Avinguda de Palma. Carrer Joan Miró and Carrer Joan Fuster lead us to Carrer Ses Oliveres, in the northwest part of the Sant Vicenç Ferrer urbanisation. At the end is an opening and a concrete path. We enter a path by its left, which climbs close to the course of the stream. The path goes in the direction of a wooded watercourse, which extends north of where we are, flanked by the coppery rocks of Na Torta. In a northern direction, we pass a gate, leaving a turning to the right and carry straight on, close to an old canal. After 10 minutes' climb we will reach a level piece of land crossed by a gully where the Font de s'Abeurada springs from.

We go back along the path, which makes a full turn, and with a steep slope and successive bends, climbs along the bottom of the watercourse until an opening: we have reached

▲ Valldemossa and, in the foreground, Sa Cartoixa ◀ Church of Sant Bartomeu ▼ Corner of Valldemossa

▲ Side of Moles de Son Ferrandell and Planícia ▼ Pla des Pouet

the Pla des Pouet, an extensive area of flat land populated by holm-oaks, with heaps of stones and ruined buildings overlooked by a well with drinking trough.

▲ Coll de Caça

GR 221 STAGE 4	SECTION 4.6 1 h

FROM PLA DES POUET TO PUIG DES CARAGOLÍ

From El Pouet we head north. We will pass alongside some large heaps of stones and some colliery huts and we enter into a rising watercourse. After a straight section, the well-defined path takes half a dozen bends and leads us to **Coll de Son Gallard** (766 m). We can see an old stone terrace as well as a *coll de tord*. The narrow pass of Son Gallard, lined by woods, frames the Punta de Sa Foradada.

The GR 221, from the coll de tord, climbs, well-defined, towards the east, close to the crest. Puig de Galatzó and the Morro d'en Fabioler stand out on the western horizon, further on than La Mola de Planícia. The refuge of Sa Talai Vella is clearly visible in the foreground, towards the northwest, as well as the adjoining coast.

After 8 minutes walking we can take (optionally) a turning to the right to visit quite an interesting spot: the Cova de s'Ermità Guillem, mainly occupied until 1635 by a venerated anchorite. Today, the cave is inhabited or conserved by someone as a place of spiritual retreat. We reach it in less than 2 minutes after passing through an opening.

Our path follows the crags and in a few more minutes we have the view of the peaks of Puig Major, Massanella and Puig Gros de Ternelles, and closer, the ridge that forms Sa Galera (908 m) and Es Teix (1.064 m). We reach a panoramic promontory (925 m) close to which we can make out, to the left and northwards, the GR turning towards the Cingles de Son Rutlan.

We can, alternatively, go as far as the small Puig des Caragolí (945 m), following the **Camí de s'Arxiduc**. This same path

▼ Sa Talaia Vella

◄ **Way of S'Arxiduc
or Es Caragolí**

also enables us to reach **Puig d'Es Teix** (1,064 m), passing by Pla de Mala Garba, where the Font de Sa Serp is (50 m). The turning towards the mountain, if we want to make the climb, is clearly marked by an exaggerated pile of stones from which we have to turn left. The path, well trodden by cattle and walkers, reaches the Pla de Mala Garba from where, by different highly visible ways, one can reach the central peak, with a magnificent panoramic view over the Serra and plain of the island.

On all this section, and on all the *Ruta de Pedra en Sec*, we will easily be able to see examples of Mallorcan goat, even the occasional male (*boc*) with considerable horns and beard. It is an autochthonous breed, traditionally hunted with dogs and snares, Its skin was once used, but today they make pies and roasts with the meat of the kids.

▲ **Wild Mallorcan goat (autochthonous breed of goat)**

▲ Sa Cova de s'Ermità Guillem   ▲ Es Caragolí   ▼ Sa Foradada

GR 221
STAGE 4

SECTION 4.7

1 h

FROM PUIG DES CARAGOLÍ TO DEIÀ, VIA THE CINGLES DE SON RUTLAN

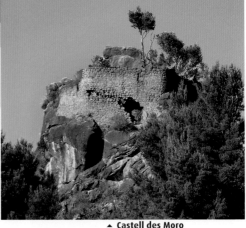

The way from the Cingles de son Rut-lan to Deià begins as a path, marked by a large heap of stones and goes along a rocky slope in the direction of a group of holm-oaks. The heaps of stones lead us to a short section of paved path that marks the beginning of the pass, a

▲ Castell des Moro

rough track also populated by holm-oaks, in the direction of Deià (NE)

The path, at the foot of the crag, drops making bends through the wood until reaching a crest that points north. We leave a turning that drops to the left (N-NW) in the di-rection of the houses of Son Rutlan. Taking the right side, after some bends, we reach a cart track. We follow it to the right until we reach a new turning —stepped— on the left that leads to a spring and the Ses Rotes cottage.

The path, stony and stepped, furrows along the watercourse in the direction of Deià (NE) and follows the gully along the right side. The path is easy and the slope gentle. We cross some land bordered by abandoned olive groves. The natural vegetation —reed, heather, mastic tree, furze, pines and wild olive— has recovered the shady space. After some curves we pass an opening and a little further on we find ourselves

▲ Es Teix

at the foot of a crag where the ruinous outline of a defence tower stands out, called **Castell des Moro** (289 m). In the background we see the peaks of Puig de Sa Galera and Punta de Sóller, alongside the sea. In a short distance the houses of Can Borràs appear, on the left. Close to the stream we pass another opening and we soon link up with a cart track that connects Can Borràs with Deià. We follow it towards the right, downhill, without leaving the main route. After a few more bends we will reach the asphalted section next to some buildings belonging to the Hotel Es Molí. Opposite, we can make out Puig de Deià, crowned by it parish church. At kilometre 62.9 we link up with the Ma-10 road. We stay on the asphalt for some 200 m to the left and at kilometre 63.1 we turn right on a downward path, also asphalted. It is Carrer des Clot which, going straight, leads us to the refuge of Can Boi, in Deià.

▲ **Can Boi refuge**

**NATURE
NOTES**

Black rockrose

Yew

Thrush

Caragol de serp

**NATURE
NOTES**

Molí de Son Mossènyer

Castell des Moro

TOWNS

VALLDEMOSSA

The current town of Valldemossa has its origin in the Islamic farmstead of Moço or Musu, which is in the old quarter. On the spot today occupied by the parish church, it is believed that there was once a mosque. The town conserves medieval reminiscences in the layout of the streets, stepped and ornamented with plants, and with a remarkable popular architecture that the tourists who vist the town really love. Valldemossa swirls around Sa Cartoixa and the church of Sant Bartomeu. The new urbanisations —which tend to occupy an increasing amount of space— have grown on the land of old country estates. Some, such as Son Gual or Sa Coma, have two defence towers. It was also the property of Archduke Louis Salvador of Hapsburg-Lorraine (1847-1915), of the Imperial Austrian house. He was a singular character, a traveller and scientist who lived on the island for many years, where he was known as S'Arxiduc. Towards the north extends the wide volume of the massif of Es Teix. The next stage runs along its westernmost spurs, along the crags of Es Caragolí and Son Rutlan, on the way to Deià.

A historical note about the Carthusian monastery of Valldemossa seems appropriate: King Jaume II of Mallorca built his fortified palace in Valldemossa (1310). The current name of this emplacement —palace of Rei Sanç (King Sancho)— corresponds to the name of Jaume II's son. In 1399, King Martí the Humane ceded it to the Carthusian monks of Sant Bru. In the mid-15th century the first church was built and in the 16th century, the second cloister and two defence towers. At the beginning of the 18th century an ambitious reform was undertaken and one hundred years later the religious orders were suppressed. The monks were finally expelled in 1835. Gaspar Melchor de Jovellanos, Chopin and George Sand, Ruben Darío, Miguel de Unamuno and Santiago Rusiñol were guests of the monastery. It is currently adapted for tourist visits. Of note are the old pharmacy, the priory cell and that of Chopin, the Baroque church, the museum with a section dedicated to S'Arxiduc, and the gardens.

PRACTICAL GUIDE

Valldemossa Town Council
Passatge Jardí de Joan Carles I, s/n
07170 Valldemossa
Tel. +34 971 61 20 02
ajuntament@valldemossa.net
Transports Illes Balears (Tib)
Tel. +34 971 17 77 77
http://tib.caib.es
Tourist and local information
www.ajvalldemossa.net
www.valldemossa.es

Valldemossa has all kinds of services. It is an almost essential tourist visit, particularly for Sa Cartoixa, for its mountainous landscape and for its popular urban architecture.

▲ **Carthusian monastery**

DEIÀ

Deià is a charming mountain village. It possesses very typical and beautiful steep narrow streets and also has some museums: that of the parish (in the church), the House-Museum of the writer Robert Graves (Ca n'Alluny), the Archaeological Museum of the Fundació Waldren… Deià has been and still is a refuge for painters, writers and musicians. Carrer des Clot, Costa d'en Topa, Carrer de Ramon Llull, the church square, surround the hill on which Deià sits. The church, with a fortifies appearance and dedicated to Saint John the Baptist, dates from the 18th century. The early parish church was destroyed by a fire in 1752. Opposite the main portal is the peculiar town cemetery, with a fabulous view. Here lie the mortal remains of Robert Graves (author of *I, Claudius*, among many other works) who lived and worked in Deià for a large part of his life. If we go down towards the road via Carrer des Puig, we will come to the Font de Sant Joan.

PRACTICAL GUIDE

Deià Town Council
Carrer des Porxo, s/n
07179 Deià
Tel. +34 971 63 90 77 / 971 63 92 33
ajuntament@ajdeia.net
Transports Illes Balears (Tib)
Tel. +34 971 17 77 77
http://tib.caib.es
Tourist and local information
www.deia-mallorca.com

Deià is a small and very touristy town, with a renowned series of restaurants. It has services of all kinds, above all during the summer. Its natural setting is really beautiful and the town itself very attractive. The abovementioned web page provides information about services and accommodation.

▲ **Deià and Puig de Sa Galera**

GR 221 **STAGE 5**

Heights

CAN MIQUELET

SECTION 5.4

SECTION 5.3

SECTION 5.5

DEIÀ

CAN BLEDA

SECTION 5.2

SECTION 5.6

SECTION 5.1

MULETA GRAN

CARRETERA

PONT DE
SA CALA

REFUGI MULETA

300 m
250 m
200 m
150 m
100 m
50 m
0 m

Distance: 10 km

Time: 3 h

Difficulty: very easy

Maps:

Instituto Geográfico Nacional 1:25.000 – number 670-III

Editorial Alpina 1:25.000 Mallorca Tramuntana Central

GR 221

3 h

Level of difficulty

5

STAGE

5

Departure
CAN BOI REFUGE
Arrival
MULETA REFUGE

‹ Llucalcari

▲ **Close to the Ses Mentides spring**

The route goes between the mountain and the sea, along the sides of the Es Teix massif. All along the way there are lots of viewpoints, ancestral homes, springs, coal silos and many other signs of an old and traditional human use of the natural resources of the Serra de Tramuntana. The path itself is the first example: its old paving, only partially preserved, has withstood the traffic of horses and cattle since the Middle Ages. Trekking, of growing importance, can contribute to recovering it.

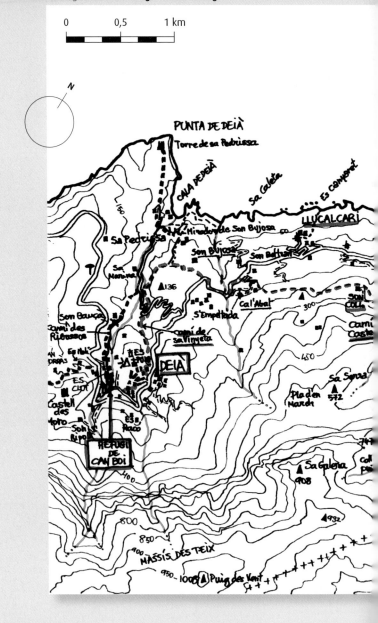

Map | 113

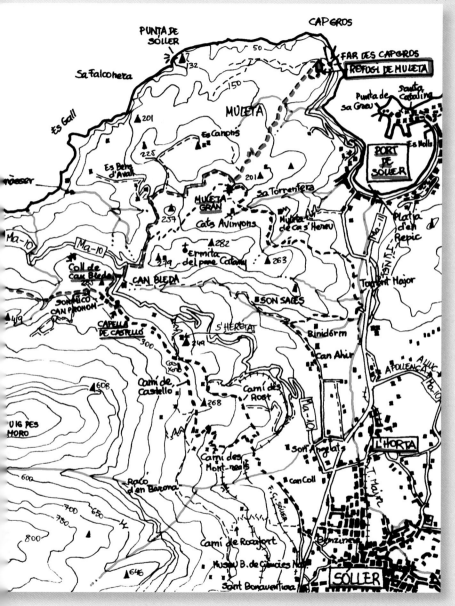

GR 221 STAGE 5	SECTION 5.1 20 mins

FROM THE REFUGE OF CAN BOI TO THE SA CALA BRIDGE

▲ Olive tree

From the refuge we return to the Ma-10 road or Carrer Arxiduc Lluís Salvador and we follow it in the direction of Sóller until almost the last houses in the town. Passing the *La Residencia* hotel, we come to the Sa Vinyeta path on the left, asphalted and well-signposted: "Sóller 2 h 30 mins / Cala de Deià 30 min". The **Sa Vinyeta path** reaches a services area, close to the school sports facilities, with a small parking space. We cross two openings.

The way becomes a paved and stepped path that winds its way down the Sa Vinyeta area, occupied by steep banks with carobs and wild olive trees and pastureland for sheep. In 5 minutes it reaches a crag from which we can see Deià below the Mola d'Es Teix (1,064 m). In front we can make out the rocky spots of Sa Pedrissa, which end at Punta de Deià, over the sea. Below us, we see the outline of the Torrent Major and that of the Camí des Ribassos path and, close to the road, the series of country houses of Son Bauçà, with an old defence tower.

The path reaches the bends of the road to the cove, promoted by Robert Graves. We will follow it downhill until coming to a crossroads, marked by the Pont de Sa Cala, a wooden way over the stream. Here begins the Camí des Ribassos towards Deià. We must cross the road, cross a gate and take the path called Sa Pesta, going uphill.

**GR 221
STAGE 5**

SECTION 5.2

25 mins

**FROM PONT DE SA CALA
TO THE DEIÀ-SÓLLER ROAD**

▲ Son Bujosa

5

We will now enter a plain which, on our left, looks over the cliff. On the other side we can see the Sa Marineta house, solitary over a large reddish crag.

Here we recommend a visit to the Son Lujosa viewpoint. To get there, we take the first turning on the left and go through a group of houses, Es Vinyet. From the viewpoint, beneath some tall pines, we can enjoy a lovely panoramic view across Cala de Deià.

From the **Son Bujosa** viewpoint, we return some eighty metres back along the path we have come by. We will reach a junction we turn to the left along the Son Bujosa way. The farmhouse appears immediately, before reaching the orchards and gardens, with cherry, orange and pear trees. A remarkably tall palm tree contrasts with the image of the rural façade. The walls of the house conceal an old defence tower.

Leaving the farmhouse on the side and without taking any turning, we continue straight on the wide way that goes through the olive grove and which, suddenly, reaches the Sóller-Deià road, close to kilometre 60.7, at the ancestral home known as S'Empeltada. Following the road to the left, after about 300 m we see the high and almost proud buildings of Ca l'Abat, overlooked by a slender defence tower.

▲ Cove of Deià

GR 221 STAGE 5	SECTION 5.3 40 mins

FROM THE DEIÀ-SÓLLER ROAD TO CAN MIQUELET

At kilometre 60.2, just before the entrance to the country estate of Son Beltran and beside the Es Roquissar house, we follow a stepped entrance,

▲ **Way of Castelló**

clearly signposted as the GR 221. The way leads to the streets of the Ses Coves de Can Puigserver urbanisation. On the left and after some curves, it recovers the original route, which we follow. We are in a mixed wood of pine trees and holm-oaks.

The path runs along a steep bank and is protected by side walls. On the left side there are several points from which to appreciate delightful views of the **Llucalcari** coastline. This village appears remote in time, with palm trees that give it an oriental air. There are three defensive towers. To the west we can still take in the headland of Deià and Es Còdols Blancs (reefs).

On a gentle, shady and slightly rising section we approach S'Esquetjar, where the way crosses the shade of a strip of crags. Almost straight, the route gradually climbs until reaching the olive groves close to Son Coll and other houses. We pass alongside the buildings.

We soon discover on the sea side the small cove of Alconàsser. After a few minutes walk along the downward path we reach a crossroads. Our way continues in the same northeast direction, conveniently signposted (Sóller 1 h 35 mins / Deià 1 h). The way passes close to the Font de Ses Mentides, an unsuspected corner. The water, used in the orchards of the Pla des Coix, springs from a small source in the slope. After a brief climb, we cross an asphalted cart track. Straight on, between walls, we pass before the houses of Can Miquelet and enter into the municipal district of Sóller.

▲ **Son Coll**

▲ Llucalcari   ▼ Marina of Deià

GR 221 STAGE 5	SECTION 5.4
	35 mins

FROM CAN MIQUELET TO CAN BLEDA

The way, well marked and with few gradients, reaches the foot of a vertical craggy spot that emerges from the wood, where there are some coal silos. A downhill pass with zigzags enables us to cross the Comellar de s'Hort Nou. After the pass —known as Es Grauet—, we reach a gate that leads to some slopes of olive groves. The way continues gently until we reach a junction.

On the right, an opening leads to the olive grove. On the left there are two ways, alongside a large plot of land. From the plot of land we can see the whole valley of Sóller and the

▲ **Son Mico**

mountainous crests that frame it: Puig de Bàlitx, Sa Bassa, Montcaire, Puig Major, the Son Torrella range, L'Ofre, Es Cornadors… Just in front there is a mound crowned by the Pi de s'Ensaimada. Our bridle path, well signposted, continues straight and converges with a cart track. If we follow it, in a few minutes we come to the avenue that the large houses of Son Mico and Can Prohom share.

Can Prohom has a façade with three levels. It features two side balconies, a way up and a series of benches. It conserves the oil press (modernised). Son Mico, a segregation of Ca Prohom, is the closest of the two farmhouses that make up the long façade. Son Mico has a remarkable rounded voussoired portal on its façade, at three heights. Around 1600 Mico was the nickname of its owner.

We pass before the façades and go alongside the gardens until reaching the **chapel of Castelló**, abandoned and at the point of becoming a ruin until not very long ago, when the Consell de Mallorca signed an agreement with the owner

Chapel of Castelló and Penyal des Migdia ▶

for its recovery. It was built around 1626 as an oratory for the large rural population of the county. With a rectangular ground plan and vaulted, with a tiled roof, it was dedicated to the Mare de Déu del Roser (Virgen of the Rosary). The façade, crowned by a simple wall belfry with a cross, has a rose window over the portal.

Making a turn, the way, now a track, drops towards the Can Bleda pass (km 56.7 of the MA-10 road). The houses of Can Bleda date back to 1511. Its defence tower and façade still give it a noble air. It is currently a rural tourism establishment. From Can Bleda you can go down to Sóller along the Son Sales path.

GR 221	SECTION 5.5
STAGE 5	30 mins

FROM CAN BLEDA TO MULETA GRAN

From the Can Bleda pass, we continue towards the left for 150 m in the direction of Deià, alongside the road. Just before the 57 km milestone, we turn right along an asphalted path that connects with Alconàsser and the Bens d'Avall urbanisation. It is a flat section that provides us with open views to-

▲ **Close to Muleta Gran**

wards the Deià coastline, with the **Punta de Sa Pedrissa** in the background. After some 300 metres, on our right we have an alternative path to go to Muleta Gran. The variant climbs up to a gully (236 m), situated very close to the Hermitage of Pare Catany, and then drops to the abovementioned country estate along the Camí de na Catanya.

The regular route, easier, continues to the bend where the

▲ **Hundred-year-old olive tree**

road begins to drop towards the sea (Bens d'Avall). On this bend we should turn to the right along a rising road that points north. After some 200 m, we should leave the main way and take a cart track (also to the right). This is the way to Muleta. More or less flat, windy and in a NE direction, in a short time it reaches the valley of Muleta, overlooked by the impressive defence tower of the houses of Muleta Gran (17th century).

The houses, of a humble appearance, seem to be half abandoned and with little activity. The country estate is made up of the "old houses" and the "new houses" and centres the valley of Muleta, closed off by the heights of Es Canons (231 m) and Serres de Muleta (291 m). The slopes are terraced and allow for agriculture, particularly olive trees. One hundred metres before reaching the entrance to the houses, on the left, we come to a turning that will lead us to the Muleta refuge.

We will return to this point at the beginning of the next stage to continue the route in the direction of Sóller.

▼ **Muleta Gran**

GR 221 **STAGE 5**	**SECTION 5.6** **30 mins**

**FROM MULETA GRAN
TO THE MULETA REFUGE**

While we are walking on we can take in the horizon silhouetted by the ranges that close off the valley of Sóller: Puig de Bàlitx, the Montcaire mountain, Puig de Sa Bassa, Puig Major, the Son Torrella range, L'Ofre, over the Biniaraix ravine, and Es Cornadors.

We climb gently in a northerly direction; in the background appears the Torre Picada at the end of the port of Sóller.

The way turns into a path and starts to drop by a rocky ridge, occupied by slopes of old smallholdings, now taken over by pine trees and attractive bushy sun spurges. We have the sea right in front of us. Shortly after crossing an old opening, we leave a turn to the right and continue on the left, on a defined way, with the remains of old paving.

The lighthouse appears after a rocky peak. We can see an electricity cable. We wind our way towards the bed of a watercourse and following the signs we first pass by a cistern and, a little further on, an old lime kiln. In the same direction as the walk, we come to a small plain with lovely views. Behind us is the crest of Alfàbia and La Mola de Es Teix.

From here a turning to the right climbs some old terraces and shortly reaches the refuge by the south façade.

The refuge occupies an old telegraph installation that was operative between 1912 and 1944. From the refuge we can go down a road for 3 km until the port of Sóller.

CAP GROS LIGHTHOUSE

This lighthouse (1842) stands over the western cliffs of the Port de Sóller. It stands 120 m high and covers a radius of 24 nautical miles. From its base, you can easily see the port, with the seafaring district of Santa Catalina, the two lighthouses on the north side of the gorge and the compact tourist buildings that occupy the contour of the beach. If you have time, you can take a boat trip from the port of Sóller along the rocky coast of the range, as far as Tuent, Sa Calobra, Formentor or the port of Pollença.

▲ **Muleta refuge**

Lighthouse of Es Cap Gros de Sóller ▸

NATURE NOTES

Ivy

White rockrose

Pine

5

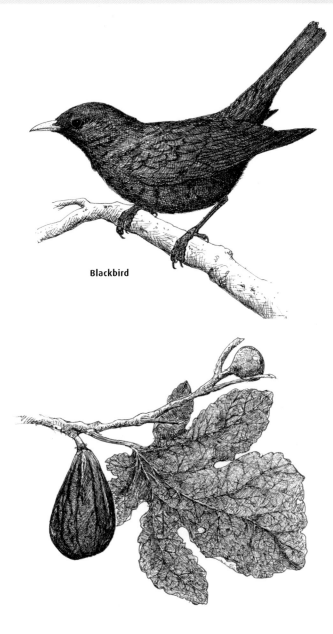

Blackbird

Fig

NATURE NOTES

Panoramic view of Es Barranc

TOWNS

PORT DE SÓLLER

The port can be reached from Sóller on the only operative tram in Mallorca, almost a relic from the past. The port is a closed and protected bay, with very crowded beaches (En Repic), and in fact it is the only safe refuge for boats on stormy days. Boats set sail from the port that take tourists along the rocky Mallorcan coast, with views of the spectacular corners and crags of the Serra de Tramuntana (Tuent, Sa Calobra, Formentor, etc.). There are excellent facilities in accommodation, shops, restaurants, banks, chemist's, etc. The Torre Picada and the oratory of Santa Caterina witnessed frequent pirate incursions in the 16th century. In May, they celebrate one of these bloody incursions into Port de Sóller with a simulated battle between "Moors" and "Christians".

PRACTICAL GUIDE

Sóller Town Council
Plaça de la Constitució, 1
Tel. 971 630 200
07100 Sóller
www.ajsoller.net
Tourist and local information
www.sollernet.com

▲ **Small lateeners in the quay**

5

▲ Port de Sóller and Puig de Bàlitx

GR 221 STAGE 6

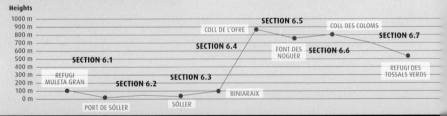

Heights

1000 m
900 m
800 m
700 m
600 m
500 m
400 m
300 m
200 m
100 m
0 m

SECTION 6.5

COLL DE L'OFRE

COLL DES COLOMS

SECTION 6.7

SECTION 6.4

FONT DES NOGUER

SECTION 6.6

SECTION 6.1

REFUGI MULETA GRAN

SECTION 6.2

SECTION 6.3

REFUGI DES TOSSALS VERDS

BINIARAIX

PORT DE SÓLLER

SÓLLER

Distance: 30 km
Time: 8 h
Difficulty: very difficult

Maps:
Instituto Geográfico Nacional 1:25.000 – numbers 670-II and 671-I
Editorial Alpina 1:25.000 Mallorca Tramuntana Central

GR 221

8 h

Level of difficulty

🥾🥾🥾🥾

6

STAGE

6

Departure

MULETA REFUGE

Arrival

TOSSALS VERDS REFUGE

‹ Torrent de Biniaraix ▲ The way of Es Barranc

This stage has two perfect complements with the optional climbs to Puig de l'Ofre and Puig des Tossals Verds. From these peaks we can see almost the entire Serra de Tramuntana while on the horizon appear Cabrera, Palma, the plain of the island, and the mountains of Artà. Moreover, the way enables us to know Sóller and its port, the Barranc de Biniaraix ravine, with its beautiful paved way, the reservoirs of Cúber and Es Gorg Blau, and some emblematic country estates, extraordinary examples of the rich natural, historical, economic and ethnological heritage of the Mallorcan mountain.

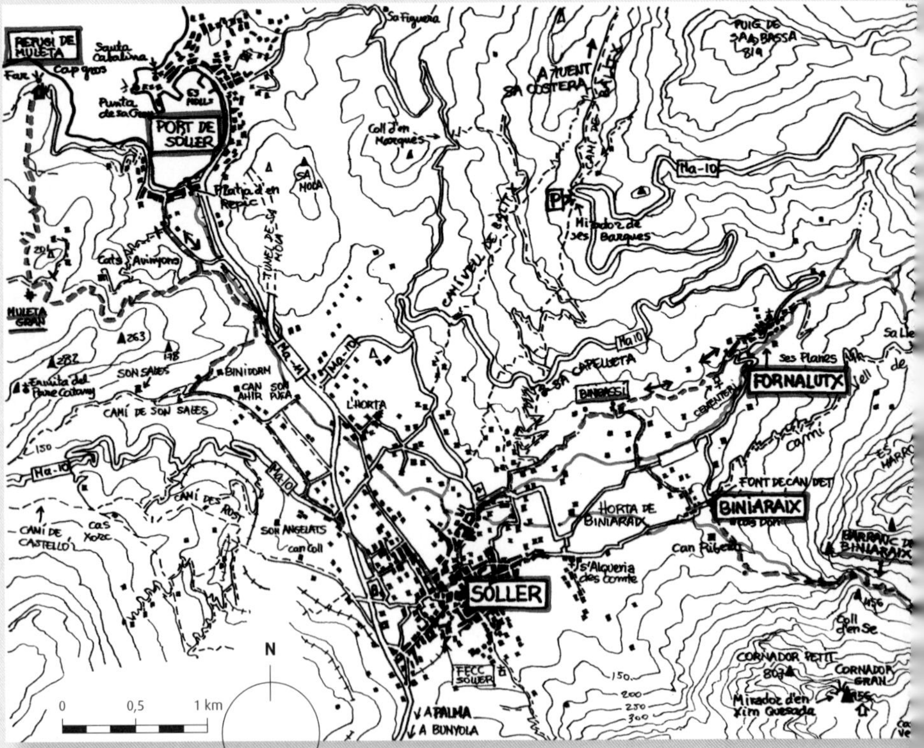
REFUGI DE MULETA
Cap gros
PORT DE SOLLER
Sa Figuera
PUIG DE SA BASSA
SA COSTERA
Coll d'en Marquès
SA MOLA
Ma-10
Mirador de ses Barques
TUNEL DE SA MOLA
CAMÍ VELL DE BALITX
MULETA GRAN
▲263
▲282
SON SALES
BINIDORM
CAN AHIR
SON PUSA
L'HORTA
SA CAPELLETA
BINIBASSÍ
FORNALUTX
Ses Planes
CEMENTERI
CAMÍ DE SON SALES
Ma-10
CAMÍ DES ROST
CAMÍ DE CASTELLÓ
SON ANGELATS
FONT DE CAN DET
BINIARAIX
HORTA DE BINIARAIX
Can Ribera
S'Alqueria des Comte
SÓLLER
BARRANC DE BINIARAIX
Coll d'en Se
CORNADOR PETIT
CORNADOR GRAN
Mirador d'en Xim Quesada
FECC SÓLLER
A PALMA
A BUNYOLA
N
0
0,5
1 km

Map | 133

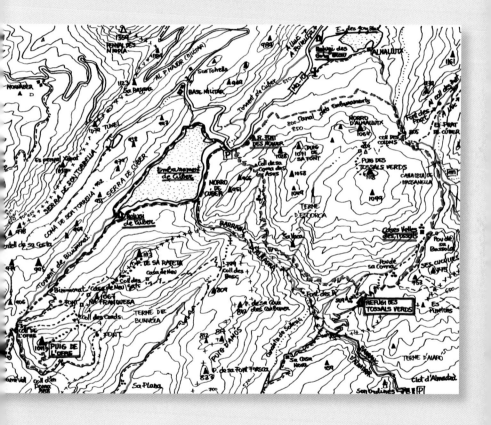

GR 221	SECTION 6.1
STAGE 6	1 h 15 mins

FROM MULETA REFUGE TO PORT DE SÓLLER

Along the same bridle path that has taken us to the refuge, we return to the houses of Muleta Gran. We will come across an information panel with directions for "Deià / Port de Sóller / Sóller". We follow the big path to the left, pass through an opening and come to a new crossroads.

▲ Way from Muleta to Port de Sóller

We must continue in the same direction we are walking, along a cart track. Some 20 metres from the crossroads, we leave it to take a turning to the right. The route turns around the south side of the country estate, from where it goes, crossing two openings with gates, towards the lands of Cas Avinyons.

In an eastern direction, and with a poorly defined path over rocks and garrigues, wild olive trees and savins, we drop down until the watercourse of Sa Torrentera. We pass the watercourse and an opening. We continue on the opposite side, climbing a hill and immediately arrive alongside the houses of Muleta de Ca s'Hereu, which we leave on our left. In the entire descent, we come across sections of beautiful paved path and stepped sections. Port de Sóller becomes an increasingly wider panoramic view.

A short drop places us in the track of the Torrent de Sa Cova. We continue on the other side of the large hillock. The garrigue, particularly in the flowering season, is a splendid show of colours and aromas: rosemary, myrtle, furze and orchids form the undergrowth of the old olive grove occupied by pine trees. Alongside an abandoned quarry, we cross a gate. The way, which is straight, passes a new fenced opening and continues along a watercourse with steep banks of olive groves.

After going downhill round some bends on one side, we join up with the path on our left that comes from the road and goes to the **beach of En Repic** in Port de Sóller. (At the time of writing, this link-up is close to the Hotel Rocamar, abandoned).

GR 221	**SECTION 6.2**
STAGE 6	**55 mins**

FROM PORT DE SÓLLER TO SÓLLER

The path from Muleta continues until Camí de Son Sales on a route that covers the lands of Binidorm. It initially follows the bank of the Torrent Major. We pass a turning to the left and walk along the flat route until we approach the houses of Son Llampaies, where we pass two small gates. A short but steep climb places us at the foot of a crag. A small protective wall presents us with an extraordinary panoramic view of the valley of Sóller and its contours.

We go down some bends and link up with a path, from Binidorm which disappears in the **Son Sales path**. The route continues on the left, on an asphalted section.

▲ **The old tram of the Port**

After passing by the houses of Ca n'Aí and passing a turning to the left —the Camí de Son Puça—, we come out on the Sóller-Deià road at km 52.75. We walk along it for about 100 metres to the right and we turn onto an asphalted road, to the left, shown with a GR sign, that comes out again on the same road.

Towards the left a roundabout is reached of the Port de Sóller to Palma ring road (Ma-11). We continue to the right for about 100 metres and enter a road on the left, shown as "Camí del Camp Llarg". We continue on the left along Carrer Cetre, pass Plaça América, and turn to the right along Carrer de Sa Mar. When this street ends, on the left, we reach Plaça de la Constitució, the central, lively and cosmopolitan part of the town.

The GR passes through the town centre ▸

▲ The valley and pass of Sóller

GR 221 STAGE 6	SECTION 6.3 55 mins

FROM SÓLLER TO BINIARAIX

From the Plaça de la Constitució, we enter Carrer de Sa Lluna. The second crossing to the left is Avinguda de la Victòria de l'11 de Maig, along which we continue our way. If we were to follow, as an option, Carrer de Sa Lluna, we would go directly to Biniaraix in about 25 minutes, crossing S'Alqueria des Comte.

▲ We leave the square behind

We continue along Avinguda Astúries as far as a bridge over the stream. Opposite is the Municipal Sports Ground and on its left the Sa Figuera way converges, which comes from Port. We will follow the asphalted way on the right, alongside the stream. In about five minutes we find ourselves before the Ca Rave bridge, with some old public washhouses.

Without crossing the bridge we follow the GR sign "Binibassí-Biniaraix 40 mins-Fornalutx 30 mins-Tuent-Sa Calobra". Opposite stands out the massive silhouette of Puig Major which here presents us with its Penya des Migdia (1,356 m). An asphalted slope, of a few hundred metres, takes us to a new junction. We continue on the right-hand side: it is the **Camí Vell de Fornalutx** or S'Ermita. Further on we see signposted to our left the turning to Sa Capelleta (Sanctuary of the Virgin María del Olivar), in Modernist style (1917). Today the Canonesses Regular of the Order of St. Augustine reside there. The sanctuary is some 500 m away along a steep short cut. It takes in adult guests, with 4 indi-

▲ Biniaraix, paved street

BINIARAIX

There used to be another Muslim farmstead in this strategic place. It conserves a characteristic structure of the medieval, mountain villages, with narrow, steep, paved streets, and beautiful traditional architecture. We should mention some stately homes such as Cas Don and Can Ribera, as well as the painted tiles of the corbel of the houses and the modest and harmonious parish church of the Inmaculada (17th century).

vidual cells, with services and shared bathroom facilities (tel.: 971 63 18 70).

From the Camí Vell de Fornalutx we can see the cultivated land of the valley and a lovely panoramic view of the Serra. We continue facing Puig Major, along the asphalted way, without turning off. The climb is gentle. We get a marvellous view of the village of Biniaraix, with the ravine in the background. We are surrounded by orchards with rich soil, populated by carob trees, citrus fruit trees, persimmons, almonds, sorbs and fig trees. Opposite, very soon, appears the group of houses of **Binibassí**. We must follow the signs. We slowly gain height as far as the houses in the village of Binibassí, with a defensive tower dating from the 16th century, reformed in the 18th. They replaced a Muslim farmstead —Benibassim or Benarrussi. They conserve some interesting painted tiles, beneath the eaves, which represent symbolic elements, and which gave protection to the inhabitants of the houses. The façade opens out to the paved courtyard though the exterior portal, a semicircular voisseured arch. As a curiosity, we can mention that it was the property, among others, of King Sancho of Mallorca, Guillem of Torrella as well as the Templar Knights.

By the left of the façade, next to the washhouses, the panel shows the way to Fornalutx. It is the start of a longer alternative to get to Lluc, adding some 30 km more. This optional route passes, after Fornalutx, the Ses Barques viewpoint, Bàlitx, Sa Costa, Sa Calobra, goes up to the Coll de Cals Reis, Son Nebot, Escorca and from here downhill to Lluc via the houses of Son Macip.

On the right, an asphalted path with the GR sign will take us, after some 500 metres, to the Ma-2121 local road from Sóller to Fornalutx. When we get there, we turn left in the direction of Fornalutx, and shortly after, we turn right for the Horta de Biniaraix path, reaching, in 10 minutes, Biniaraix.

▲ Small tavern in Biniaraix

GR 221 STAGE 6	SECTION 6.4 1 h 50 min.

FROM BINIARAIX TO COLL DE L'OFRE

From the small square of the parish church we take Carrer Sant Josep. Before the country house of Cas Don we leave the turning to our left, suitable for vehicles, which comes from Fornalutx. Passing the turning we will come to a small square with the washhouses fed with water from the Font d'en Det. We see two ways. One, asphalted and rising, is the old Monnàber way, a country estate located at the foot of Puig Major. The one on the right, flat and indicating "L'Ofre-Barranc de Biniaraix-Lluc", marks the way to follow.

▲ Ses Voltetes

If we look back we will have wonderful views over the orchards of Biniaraix and the village. The path very soon reaches the stream and crosses it, and begins the climb to the heart of the ravine. After a few paved bends, it reaches a small spring. A few minutes after a turning to the right, after a flat section, we reach a junction, alongside a carob tree and just before the second bridge.

We have the option of following on the right the Camí Vell des Barranc, by the Coll d'en Se, a route that avoids the bed of the ravine, gaining in views. The usual, and classic, route penetrates the **S'Estret** area, channelled between rocky walls and right by the stream.

The Barranc de Biniaraix is almost a geological virtuosity that has its origin in the alpine contraction stage that occurred some 20 million years ago. The old stone path, which runs for 3.5 km and made up of some 2,000 steps, leads us to the deep valley of Ofre, overlooked by the unmistakable rock formation of the mountain of the same name.

▲ Old washhouses

◀ ▾ Gorges and stepping stones in the stream

As we climb, the ravine way enables us to see the valley of Sóller and the port.

After almost an hour of climbing the houses of Can Silles are reached, of sober architecture, like their neighbours, Can Sivella. They are surrounded by steep slopes of orchards. The path that goes alongside it —which we do not take— climbs along Coma des Verger as far as Coma de Son Torrella, a karstic, sunken valley of singular beauty.

The Camí des Barranc, after the Es Verger turning, meets up with the way on the right that comes from Coll d'en Se, and immediately starts a long and winding climb to reach the foot of the Coves d'en Mena and a little further on the Salt des Cans, from where the spectacular precipice of the **Torrent de l'Ofre** is clearly visible, particularly if water is flowing. We reach the opening to the Ofre plain, visible from an adjoining piece of flat land. A path leaves from here, on our left, which climbs back up a slope and comes out on a bend of the track which, from the right comes from the houses.

L'Ofre (in the past, Lofra) has its origins in a Muslim farmstead, —balhofra— and has two sets of houses, the new ones and the old ones. Close to the houses springs the Font de Sa Teula. The houses and the spring are on private property.

We see remains of the old, paved, bridle path, which enables us to cut the wide bends of the track that climbs to the Coll de l'Ofre.

PUIG DE L'OFRE

The climb (optional) to the peak of Puig de l'Ofre (1,093 m) can take some 45 mins. From the pass we have to go back a little along the track that drops to the houses of Ofre, and turn onto another track that we will find on the left. Coll d'en Poma and the wall that crosses it will show us the beginning of the path that climbs to the peak on our left. The track we have come along as far as Coll d'en Poma continues and drops to the Comasema valley and other possibilities open up for us such as the Vall d'Orient and even the Castell d'Alaró.

The numerous piles of stones will help us reach the peak without any orientation problems. If you do not want to go back down along the same path, we can take its NE crest, towards Coll des Cards, and from here descend some 150 m, going northwards, until the wide path that drops from Coll de l'Ofre to the Cúber reservoir.

▲ **Black vulture**

▲ Puig de l'Ofre

◀ ▼ Details of dry stone masonry

GR 221 STAGE 6	SECTION 6.5 1 h

FROM COLL DE L'OFRE TO THE FONT DES NOGUER

▲ **Puig Major**

Coll de l'Ofre is an open spot with a panoramic view, distinguishable for the conical silhouette of the mountain (1,093 m). From the Coll de l'Ofre we must follow the GR signs, which show us a short cut downhill. After about 10 minutes we recover the wide path on out right. The streambed comes from the Font de s'Aritja, which springs from beneath some black poplars higher up from the houses of Binimorat. They are austere houses that overlook the lands of the old Islamic farmstead, documented in the 13th century and dedicated to livestock.

A great landscape surrounds us. To the north we can identify the Cúber mountain chain. To the east, the peaks of Na Franquesa (1,067 m) and Sa Rateta (1,113 m). Opposite are the much-admired **Puig Major** and **Puig de ses Vinyes**, profiles that will accompany us for a large part of the route. Cows and sheep and the occasional donkey graze freely close to the way. The place is good for observing birds of prey: booted eagle, kite, cinereous vulture and falcon. We go through an opening. Around us we discover lots of huts —constructions that shelter the livestock—, the majority of them in ruins. This county, like others in the Mallorcan mountains, once had a great deal of livestock activity. In summer the flocks and herds from the country estates on the plain and the south of the island arrived, where there was usually a shortage of water and food during the dry months.

The valley extends out. One kilometre further on a closed gate forces us to pass though another gate for walkers, ten steps to the left. Further on, a short detour to the left leads to the Cúber refuge, owned by the government of the Balearic Islands (tel.: 900 300 001). This refuge is a restored hut, with a

▲ Way from L'Ofre to Cúber   ▼ Cúber reservoir

6

capacity for eight people; it has drinking water, WC, wood, chimney, 8 bunk beds, tables and chairs, and selective rubbish containers. It is 1.5 kilometres from the Ma-10 road.

There are two ways of getting there. The first follows the wide, asphalted way towards the **dam of the Cúber** reservoir and after 15 minutes walk links up over a gate with the road at kilometre 34. The reservoir dates from 1971. The second way follows the GR sign, which leads us to the flat path that borders the reservoir on the north bank, at the foot of the Serra de Cúber. The calm water feeds the fish introduced here for freshwater fishing. The area is visited by many gulls, ospreys and cormorants. Sa Rateta and Morro de Cúber (951 m) are reflected in the water. Before being abandoned and flooded, Cúber was a cold, but fertile valley, overlooked by large houses. Of Romanesque origin, Quelber or Quber would be the old spelling of Cúber.

At last we reach the road barrier, where there is a small car park. Without crossing it, we continue alongside the fence, on the right, until a step in a wall leaves us in the recreational area of Font des Noguer, an enclosed space close to the road (km 33.7 of the Ma-10), where the fountain springs from. There are tables, benches and barbecue facilities.

The road continues downhill and after 2 km passes by another refuge, that of Gorg Blau. It has the same characteristics as the Cúber refuge and gets its name from the nearby reservoir.

▲ Orchid

▲ Weasel

GR 221
STAGE 6

SECTION 6.6
55 mins

6

FROM FONT DES NOGUER
TO COLL DES COLOMS

VARIANT

FROM FONT DES NOGUER
TO THE TOSSALS VERDS
REFUGE VIA THE PAS LLIS
Page 154

Alongside the road we can see the cement canal that through pumping and decanting takes the excess water from the Es Gorg Blau to the Cúber reservoir. In accordance with the signs, we start the walk in a NE direction, alongside the abovementioned canal. In a few minutes, we will enjoy great panoramic views of the Almallutx plain with the **Gorg Blau reservoir**, overlooked by the massif of Puig Major (1,436 m) and its smaller brother, Puig de ses Vinyes (1,108 m). Further east the Puig de Massanella stands out (1,365 m) and the Serra des Teixos (1,259 m): part of the stage runs between them. The first part of the route is in the shadow of the abrupt crest made up of the Morro de Cúber (951 m), Puig de Sa Font (1,071 m) and the Morro d'Almallutx (1,064 m).

The predominant vegetation adapts to this setting of extreme climate, as well as to the arid soil and the actions of animals and man. We see common species (furze, reed, pine, blackberry, *estepa joana –Hypericum balearicum–* or St Johnswort, euphorbia) and others not so abundant (rushes, orchids, *estepa blenera –Phlomis italica* or Balearic island sage).

We pass several stream beds and leave three bridges that cross the canal behind us. After about 20 minutes we are in the shadow of Morro d'Almallutx. Alongside the reservoir we recognise the estate of Almallutx. The path changes direction towards the Coll des Coloms. When the canal crosses the stream, we cross it via a small concrete bridge.

We enter into a holm-oak wood and progress quite steeply on the right side of the watercourse. The way is paved in some sections and straight. We pass a stone opening, go around some silos and finally reach the Coll des Coloms (808 m), a natural pass towards the south side of the Serra.

GR 221 STAGE 6	SECTION 6.7
	1 h 10 mins

FROM COLL DES COLOMS TO THE TOSSALS VERDS REFUGE

▲ Arches of Sa Canaleta

We continue in the same direction and after some 150 m we make out a turning to the right, shown as Puig des Tossals. In 40 minutes, following a path, we reach a pass that enables the ascension of Morro d'Almallutx (1,064 m) or Puig des Tossals Verds (1,118 m). It is optional. The same sign shows us the route to follow to the refuge, SE: "Refugi Tossals Verds, 1 h 5 mins".

We follow a short section, in a reasonable state of conservation, and after a couple of bends we come to a fork. The left fork is the continuation of the GR towards Lluc (next stage). The right fork, straight, goes to the abovementioned refuge. This way, well defined and flat or downhill, always with beautiful paving, runs along the slopes of the Torrent des Prat ravine until it reaches the plain and encounters the remains of the **Ses Cases Velles des Tossals** estate. Following the same path, in less than half an hour it drops to the Tossals Verds refuge, run by the Consell de Mallorca, in the public estate of Es Tossals Verds, 578 hectares, situated on the southern boundary of the Escorca municipal district. The houses overlook a low ridge of steep banks and areas of olive groves, where some prehistoric constructions are preserved.

CASTELL D'ALARÓ

The visit to the Castell d'Alaró from the Tossals Verds refuge takes 3 hours but enables us to gain a different perspective of the Serra de Tramuntana. At he same time, history and legend will provide added value to our walk.

We go down the asphalted path that reaches the refuge and along some sections of the old paved way. At the same point where the path reaches the Torrent d'Almadrà we turn along the path on the right, towards a small bridge and a wall. It is the entrance to country estates of Sa Casa Nova and Solleric, private properties, separated by the Coll de Sa Corona.

Once in Solleric, we link up with the Ma-2100 road. Towards the right, going eastwards, we must go along 2.5 km of asphalted way to reach kilometre 11.8. We will come across a path to the left

▲ Tossals Verds refuge

that climbs to the Pla des Pouet (700 m). From here, a well signposted paved bridle way takes us on the last section of the climb to the castle.

Before entering into the walled precinct of the castle, on the right we meet up with the path that comes from the village of Alaró. A little further on, behind the semicircular arch of a tower, we just have a short climb remaining that passes close to the vertical and impressive north face of Puig d'Alaró (821 m), and which goes as far as the hostelry and oratory, dedicated to the Mare de Déu del Refugi (Virgin of the Refuge) and built in 1622. The place has a long tradition of hermitages.

The history of this castle goes further back than the Roman occupation. It was a stronghold of Muslim resistance against the forces of King Jaume I, who occupied it in 1231. The small Baroque chapel recalls the figures of Cabrit and Bassa, defenders of the castle in the siege by the Catalan-Aragonese troops of Alfonso the Liberal, who confronted King Jaume II. Cabrit and Bassa, defeated, were condemned to death by being burnt at the stake.

To reach the castle, the *Ruta de pedra en sec* passes along the Camí Vell d'Orient. This path leaves from the same estate in a southerly direction, borders the Torrent de Solleric, and links up with the Ma-2100 road, close to the km 18 post. After some 400 metres of asphalt, and now in sight of the village of Alaró, the classic path that climbs to the castle leaves on the right.

▾ **Alaró Castle**

▲ The valley of Solleric from Alaró Castle

GR 221 STAGE 6	VARIANT 2 h 30 mins

FROM FONT DES NOGUER TO THE TOSSALS VERDS REFUGE VIA THE PAS LLIS

FROM FONT DES NOGUER TO PAS LLIS
1 h 30 mins

▲ Pas Llis or Es Forellat

From Font des Noguer (km 33.7 of the Ma-10 road), we return by where we have come from and after crossing the fence we come to a cross wall. Whereas the GR continues in the direction of the Cúber reservoir, the Pas Llis way, which requires prudence, turns and climbs alongside the abovementioned wall, with a steep slope and continuous bends, until the pass that leads to the entrance to **La Coma des Ases** (903 m), between the Morro de Cúber and Puig de Sa Font. The area was subjected, rather unsuccessfully, to a reforestation process.

The pass is enclosed by a long wall. We go through an opening and begin the descent of Sa Coma des Ases, a tributary of the Torrent d'Almadrà. The southern slopes of Puig de Sa Font close the low ridge on the left. Some bends lead us to the track of the watercourse. Towards the south we identify the silhouettes of Puig d'Amós, Puig de S'Alcadena and the castle of Alaró, as well as the spots of the Pla and, even further, the massif of Cura.

By the left side of the low ridge we reach the top of a hill (800 m) and then continue down along the watercourse until a flat area with an old plot of land and a tumbledown hut.

We continue along a mountainside with a steep gradient. After passing a rocky ridge, we reach the bottom of another streambed, at the foot of a large section of steep ground. The narrow path winds its way down until a pass that crosses a crest. We go along a cliff between the crags and ravine of the **Torrent d'Almadrà** to climb towards the Pas Llis, once known as Pas des Forellat. It is a little slippery, but thanks to a safety handrail, does not represent any difficulty.

FROM PAS LLIS
TO THE TOSSALS VERDS REFUGE
1 h

We continue parallel to the ravine, going up and down successively. We cross a rough ravine and dominated by an impressive spur, the Morro de Sa Vaca. The way becomes smoother and flatter again. We overcome an eroded crest and cross another watercourse. On the adjoining hill we can now make out the refuge; a coal silo leads to a bridle path that leads to the opening to the olive grove.

The path, winding, crosses Sa Coma, covered with steep slopes and leads to a pass with an opening, alongside Es Putxol (569 m). We drop down to a low wooden gate that enables access to the refuge.

▾ **Puig de sa Font**

**NATURE
NOTES**

Osprey

Partridge

Alaró Castle

TOWNS

SÓLLER

The valley of Sóller is a unique spot on the island of Mallorca, closed between mountains (Serra d'Alfàbia, l'Ofre, Es Cornadors…), with a landscape that combines proportionally rouge crags, olive trees, the town, the orange orchards, the tiny villages of Fornalutx and Biniaraix and rural paths. Sóller is a big tourist attraction and has all services (accommodation, transport to Palma, banks, shops, hotels and restaurants, medical attention, chemist's, etc.). It is also a centre from which irradiate beautiful paths for walkers, with different levels of length and difficulty. The town's civil buildings are of great interest, some of them built by emigrants from Sóller who returned to the town after becoming quite rich abroad (France, above all), or by busy textile industrialists at the beginning of the 20th century (see the streets called Sa Lluna, Gran Via, Hospici, Sant Nicolau, etc.). The traditional architecture of narrow streets combines with the character left behind by Modernism, coinciding with moments of splendour for the city. A stroll around its streets must include the visit to the railway station, to the parish church of Sant Bartomeu (a mixture of Baroque, neoclassical and Modernist styles with origins in the 13th century), to the Banc de Sóller (a beautiful building with a Modernist façade by the architect Joan Rubió, also author of part of the parish church), to the Plaça de la Constitució and the Natural Science Museum with a small, peaceful botanical garden of Balearic flora (Can Pruaga).

PRACTICAL GUIDE

Sóller Town Council
Plaça de la Constitució, 1
07100 Sóller
Tel. +34 971 63 02 20
ajuntament@a-soller.es
Transports Illes Balears (Tib)
Tel. +34 971 17 77 77
http://tib.caib.es
Tren de Sóller (railway)
www.trendesoller.com
Tourist and local information
www.ajsoller.net
http://a-soller.tiscalibiz.com

Sóller has all kinds of facilities. It is a very lively town with a high level of tourism throughout the year. The visit to the Port de Sóller is highly recommendable (tram). The websites mentioned provide very complete information about the services, shops, accommodation and cultural activities of the town.

▲ Plaça de Sóller

▲ Square in Sóller

GR 221 STAGE 7

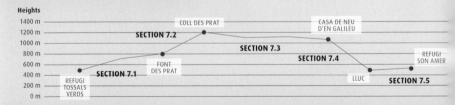

Heights

1400 m
1200 m — SECTION 7.2
1000 m
800 m
600 m
400 m — REFUGI TOSSALS VERDS — SECTION 7.1
200 m
0 m

COLL DES PRAT

CASA DE NEU D'EN GALILEU

SECTION 7.3

SECTION 7.4

FONT DES PRAT

REFUGI SON AMER

LLUC

SECTION 7.5

Distance: 16 km

Time: 5 h 15 min.

Difficulty: difficult

Maps:

Instituto Geográfico Nacional 1:25.000 - number 671-I

Editorial Alpina 1:25.000 Mallorca Tramuntana Nord

GR 221

5 h 15 mins Level of difficulty

✎✎✎✎

STAGE

7

Departure
TOSSALS VERDS REFUGE
Arrival
SON AMER REFUGE

‹ **Autumn in the range**   ▲ **Puig Major**

The way now crosses the heart of the Serra de Tramuntana: the limestone mountain with the almost aesthetic effects of erosion in many places, snow huts, the sea always on the horizon, sometimes calm and other times rough and dark, the wide panoramic views towards the Pla and the Llevant, and beyond... It is the time for walking between solitary naked peaks and long ridges covered with reed grass, and for going over unsuspected passes and along old but well restored paths. And if that were not enough, the big Mallorcan mountains such as Puig Major, Massanella, Puig de l'Ofre, Penyal d'Es Migdia, Es Tossals, En Galileu and others rise around the monastery of Lluc, which tradition considers to be the spiritual centre of Mallorca, bountiful in legends.

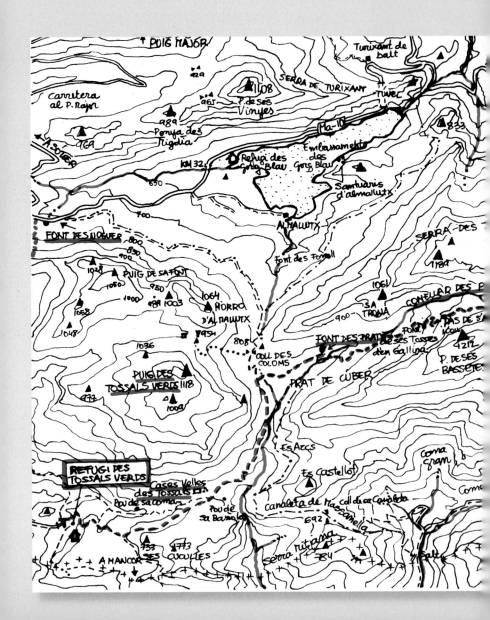

Map | 163

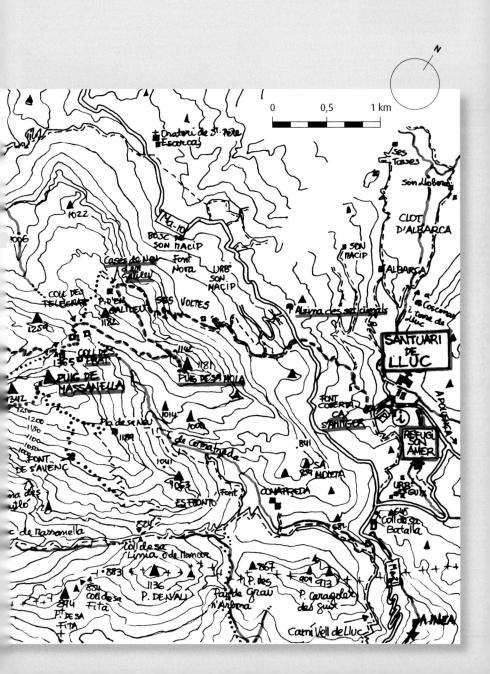

GR 221 STAGE 7	SECTION 7.1 1 h

FROM THE TOSSALS VERDS REFUGE TO FONT DES PRAT DE MASSANELLA

▲ **Es Tossals**

We leave the Tossals Verds refuge in a NE direction (on the same path used on the variant that went over the Coll des Coloms from Font des Noguer), crossing a wooden gate. We continue along an old bridle path that gradually climbs to cross an olive grove, today invaded by reeds. In 5 minutes a path turns off to the left that leads to Pou de Sa Coma. We carry on to the right, beside a rebuilt collier's hut and its circular silo. To the west we can see the refuge, the outlines of the mountains of Alcadena and the Castell d'Alaró and the Orient valley. On our left rises the rough south face of Es Tossals and facing us, the head of Puig de Massanella. We walk alongside an old canal, now piped, which comes from Font des Prat. After having passed an opening in the wall, we reach a pass (650 m) where we see the way to Pinatons signposted and which leads, via Es Rafals, to the village of Mancor de la Vall.

We continue in a NE direction along the west side of Ses Cuculles (747 m), along a section of path that climbs gently, in the shadow of tall pine trees. Passing another opening we see the plain of Ses Cases Velles, with the ruins of the country estate. Behind them stand some curious rock formations, known popularly as Ses Capelletes. We leave a path on our right and in a few minutes reach the plain. To our right is Pou de Sa Bassola, of rustic architecture.

We continue along the route and, at the end of an enclosure, we enter the wood. We cover a paved section that borders the crags of Torrent des Prat. On our right we discover **Es Arcs**, part of a small aqueduct (**Sa Canaleta**) built in the 18th century by Monserrat Fontanet, which channels the water from the Font des Prat to the Massanella estate and, in recent times, to the town of Mancor. At the level of a new opening

▲ Ses Cases Velles

▲ Es Prat spring

we notice, on the opposite bank, a constructive relic: Es Molinot, an old watermill. Over stepping stones and a wooden bridge, we cross the torrent twice. We continue along the left of the watercourse and shortly reach a junction with a sign that says "Font des Noguer 55 mins / Font des Prat 10 mins / Lluc 4 h". At this point we link up with the path that arrives from Font des Noguer along the canal that comes from the reservoirs of Cúber and Es Gorg Blau and from the Coll des Coloms.

We walk along the right-hand turning, sufficiently defined. The narrow path runs through the wood, passes alongside an enclosure and reaches a junction. We have the Font des Prat opposite, a short distance away, at the foot of a rocky place, in a dry masonry wall in the shadow of a large holm-oak. The well is very old and has the name of Font de Massanella inscribed. When it rains it carries a large flow.

GR 221 STAGE 7	SECTION 7.2 1 h 30 mins

FROM FONT DES PRAT TO THE COLL DES PRAT OR SES CASES DE NEU

▲ **Puig de ses Bassetes**

We regain the path and continue following the signs of the GR 221 along a very clear path that climbs the eastern sides of the hillock. The first section of the climb crosses a shady holm-oak wood with frequent remains of coal silos. Passing an opening, on the left we have a good vantage point to see back over where we have come from. With a continuous gradient and bends, we enter into an area of mixed wood, and reach the **Font de ses Tosses d'en Gallina**, with a humble drinking trough, at an altitude of approximately 950 m.

On reaching an area with large pine trees on the left we can make out the formidable Serra des Teixos, with a separated crag: Sa Trona (1,061 m). Opposite appears the pass and further to the right the peaks of Puig de Massanella (1,365 m) and Puig de ses Bassetes (1,212 m), separated by the Coll de n'Argentó. The gradient is gentle and we move into open country. On our right we see a demolished hut. Around appear banks of dry-stone walls where we find a snow hut.

▲ **Honeysuckle**

▲ **Mountain orchid**

PUIG DE MASSANELLA

Puig de Massanella (1,365 m) is the highest peak in Mallorca which you can climb without asking for special permits, because Puig Major (1,445 m) is occupied by a surveillance station of the Spanish Air Defence system. The optional climb to Massanella will take us some 50 minutes and covers, to a large extent, a private estate that charges to go through it. From the demolished hut, a narrow path leaves that leads to the Coll de n'Argentó (1,158 m), close to which is another snow hut. From this pass you can climb, without a path, following the piles of stones that seek out the south side of Massanella, where the gradient is less steep. From the Coll de n'Argentó we also have the choice of making the climb, in a northeast direction, directly via the scarped crest. Whether by one side or the other, after having surpassed a first peak, in 10 minutes we reach the highest part of the Mola del Massanella.

We cover the last slope of the Comellar des Prat and with a little effort we will come to the Coll des Prat (1,205 m), bordered by a large enclosing wall, on the right, as far as the foot of the impressive precipices of Massanella. This environment is rich in endemic species of mountain flora such as the Massanella sun spurge, or the selfsame maçanella (stinking camomile) which gives its name to the mountain.

Facing us the countryside opens out towards the bays in the north (Alcúdia and Pollença) and, behind, we can appreciate a large part of the western Serra. Puig Major stands out clearly. In the background, we can make out Puig de Galatzó.

▾ **Serra des Teixos**

GR 221 STAGE 7	**SECTION 7.3** 1 h 15 mins

FROM COLL DES PRAT TO CASA DE NEU D'EN GALILEU

A new sign, "Casa de neu d'en Galileu / Lluc 2 h 30 mins" marks the route northwards. It climbs until the adjoin-

▲ Lichen

ing crest via a simple pass and we drop to the nearby snow hut and in 5 more minutes reach the **Coll des Telègraf** (1,126 m), identified by two snow huts, on either side with huts.

The *Ruta de pedra en sec* drops eastwards towards the snow hut and, after a short descent, crosses the Comellar de Comafreda and climbs as far as Coll d'en Galileu, leaving Puig de Sa Mola (1,181 m) or Puig d'en Galileu to the right. This peak probably provides the very best views of the county. A signposted path will lead us in twenty minutes to the plain where there is an interesting example of snow hut.

LES CASES DE NEU

Of the dozen snow huts that are known in this area, one of them is currently the object of a restoration programme. It is the snow hut of En Galileu, situated at 1,090 m altitude and made up of a snow hut and building, as well as steep slopes and a water well. The snow hut is elliptical in shape, lined by dry stone masonry walls and with facings that support a tiled gable roof. It is 14 metres long, 7 wide and 6 deep. At one end the doorway is conserved, and at the other end, a hole where the snow was shovelled into, called *bombardera* (loophole). The building, now roofless, was divided into two rooms.

The medicinal and gastronomic uses of snow are documented since Antiquity in different cultures. In Mallorca, the first reference to obtaining ice from snow appears in 1564. From then until the early 20th century, when ice was by then obtained through industrial means, the collecting and conservation of snow depended on installations called cold rooms, always located in high and cold spots of our mountains, where snowfall was frequent in winter. Huts and paths facilitated the collection and transporting of the snow, duly protected, with mules and carts as far as the villages and to Ciutat de Mallorca (Palma).

7

▲ Coll des Telègraf ▼ Snow hut

GR 221 STAGE 7	SECTION 7.4 1 h 15 mins

FROM CASA DE NEU D'EN GALILEU TO LLUC

▲ **Basilica of Lluc**

Close to the constructions, we find the snow hut path that drops to the wood of Son Macip. It is known as the **Camí de ses Voltes d'en Galileu** due to its spectacular route. It has recently been recovered by workers of the Environmental Department of the Consell de Mallorca with the help of European funding.

Very soon, the old bridle path, paved and protect by a side wall, is furrowed by a pass, which is a dizzying vantage point. With lots of bends, the downhill walk begins, except for several hillocks and crags. The wood spreads out beneath us until it merges with the olive grove, at a lower altitude.

At the foot of the crags, the path becomes a track. After about 10 minutes we leave a turning on the left. Shortly after, we continue the way on the right that further on crosses a wall to reach the Ma-10 road, close to km 22.5. We cross the road, reach a small area of flat land with coal silos and we continue beneath the canopy of the wood. The path is paved, winding and downhill. From some of the bends we can take in the splendid scenery in which Puig Roig, Puig Caragoler de Femenia and, in the background, Puig Gros de Ternelles, all stand out. To the right is Moleta de Binifaldó and Puig Tomir.

The bridle path crosses two consecutive openings at the same time leaving two turnings to the left. One of them corresponds to the variant of the previous stage that comes from Binibassí and Fornalutx on a route closer to the sea.

In a short distance, we pass close to a curve of a track that we should not follow. Our route carries on in the same direction among pine trees, holm-oaks, olive trees and rockroses. We will reach an opening that leads to the group of white poplars where Font Coberta is.

7

▲ ▼ **Bends in En Galileu**

▲ **Son Macip wood**   ▼ **Towards Lluc**

On our right, and just before the restaurant, is the spring, the star of many popular stories. It is said that Francesc Sa Coma, in 1334, gave it to the monastery so that monks and pilgrims could use its water. It was then known as Font des Pi. They say that a settler in the 16th century wanted to cut off the supply. The spring dried up, but a new jet of water appeared on the land owned by the monks, an event considered miraculous. It is traditionally accepted that its curative properties for stomach pains are authentic. An image of the Virgin Mary at the end of a shady passage protects the spring.

From the spring we can drop down to the square of the monastery of Lluc, crossing the car park. After this, to the right, are the houses of Ca S'Amitger (Information Centre of the Serra de Tramuntana).

GR 221 STAGE 7	SECTION 7.5
	15 mins

FROM LLUC TO THE SON AMER REFUGE

▲ **Holm-oak**

Having visited Lluc we can return to Ca s'Amitger and continue alongside the road that links up with the Ma-10, until an opening on the right where we take the path to the Son Amer Refuge. After some 400 m we can make out in the fields on the right the Lluc watermill, used in the past to grind cereals for flour. We pass a gated opening, cross a wide path and continue along a paved path that climbs the hill where the houses of Son Amer are situated. In the 13th century, Son Amer formed part of the farmstead of Puig Ferrer, more extensive and in the hands of the

▲ ▼ **Monastery of Lluc**

▲ Lluc and Puig Roig

▲ **Son Amer refuge**

Templar Knights. In the 15th century, it became the property of the Amer family, landowners closely linked to Inca. The building, of an austere appearance, conserves the body of the old defence tower. It dominates the whole setting of Lluc. The refuge (on an estate of 103 hectares) has a walkers' information centre.

CAMÍ VELL DE LLUC

From Font Coberta an asphalted road leads, in a series of bends, to Coll de Sa Batalla, a crossroads with ways to Sóller, Pollença and Inca. Going over the pass by road in the direction of Inca and just past the stone bridge over the Torrent des Guix, by an opening on the right, a track forms the continuation of the Camí Vell de Lluc, a medieval way well signposted for walkers.

It is a gentle route with good panoramic views. We reach the village of Caimari in nearly two hours. It is an emblematic path for the infinite number of pilgrims who since the 13th century have climbed and continue climbing to the monastery. In Caimari it is where different "Lluc ways" converge, originating from nearly all the towns of Mallorca.

Currently, the Camí Vell de Lluc forms part of the second Grand Rondonée promoted by the Consell de Mallorca, the Ruta Artà-Lluc or GR 222.

NATURE NOTES

Finch

Painted lady butterfly

Wood pigeon

NATURE NOTES

Mola d'en Galileu

Dry stone masonry wall

Bastard balm

Honeysuckle

Snow hut (Massanella)

TOWNS

LLUC

The monastery is today more a tourist attraction than any-thing else, an unbeatable excursion centre located in the heart of the Serra. It has an interesting museum with collections of lavish arts, archaeology, popular ceramics and painting. In the monastery square you can buy souvenirs of a religious or ethnological nature and books that contain the history of the place or the many legends starring the Virgin or *Mare de Déu de Lluc*. You should not forget that in the monas-tery square is the Escorca town hall building, the municipal district in which Lluc is located. In Lluc you can spend the night (the monastery rents out cells), on the condition that you book in advance, because a lot of people spend days in the monastery to both satisfy their religious concerns and to rest or walk around its privileged setting. From Lluc you can climb to the peaks of Massanella and Tomir, go around Puig Roig (through the Mossa and Es Cosconar estates), go down (with great care and well equipped and guided) to the Tor-rent de Pareis as far as Sa Calobra, and go on other trips. In Lluc it is possible to see snow in winter. Believers can pray to the Virgin Mary: the place is a setting for popular religious-ness. The children of the *escolanía*, the trainee acolytes of the monastery, *Blauets*, sing in the religious services, above all on Christmas Eve (24 December).

PRACTICAL GUIDE

Escorca Town Council
Plaça dels Pelegrins, 9
07315 Escorca
Tel. +34 971 51 70 05
Transports Illes Balears (Tib)
Tel. +34 971 17 77 77
http://tib.caib.es
Tourist and local information
www.ajescorca.net
Information about the Sanctuary of Lluc
www.lluc.net

Paradoxically, Escorca is the largest district of Mallorca and the least populated. The town hall is in the square that welcomes the pilgrims that visit the sanctuary of Lluc, which is an absolute must for all the hikers who cross the Serra de Tramuntana. There is accommodation in the sanctuary, and in the square there are cafeterias, restaurants and food shops and shops selling products made in the sanctuary or the area. Ca s'Amitger (leaving the square) is the Information Centre for the Serra de Tramuntana.

▲ **Detail of the Way of the Cross**

▲ Interior of the Basilica of Lluc

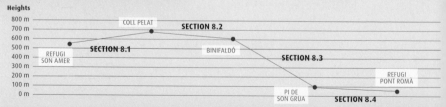

GR 221 STAGE 8

Heights

COLL PELAT
SECTION 8.2
REFUGI SON AMER
SECTION 8.1
BINIFALDÓ
SECTION 8.3
REFUGI PONT ROMÀ
PI DE SON GRUA
SECTION 8.4

Distance: 17 km

Time: 4 h 45 min.

Difficulty: easy

Maps:

Instituto Geográfico Nacional 1:25,000 - numbers 671-I, 644-III and 644-IV

Editorial Alpina 1:25.000 Mallorca Tramuntana Nord

GR 221

4 h 45 mins

Level of difficulty

🥾🥾🥾

8

STAGE
8

Departure
SON AMER REFUGE
Arrival
PONT ROMÀ REFUGE

◄ **Es Bosc Gran**   ▲ **Winter ascent**

The eighth stage of the *Ruta de pedra en sec* is bidding farewell to an unforgettable experience. Pollença, with many unique living traditions, welcomes hikers who have wanted to discover Mallorca with an effort and far from the tourist clichés. The stage is gentle and allows for intimate moments to savour the last taste of the Mallorcan mountain. We will pass close to the big country estates of the range, will have the option to go off the *Ruta de pedra en sec* to go on a rugged climb up Puig Tomir, perhaps one of the most beautiful viewpoints over the Serra de Tramuntana, and we will frequently be walking over the old way where there are no lack of Roman heaps of stones.

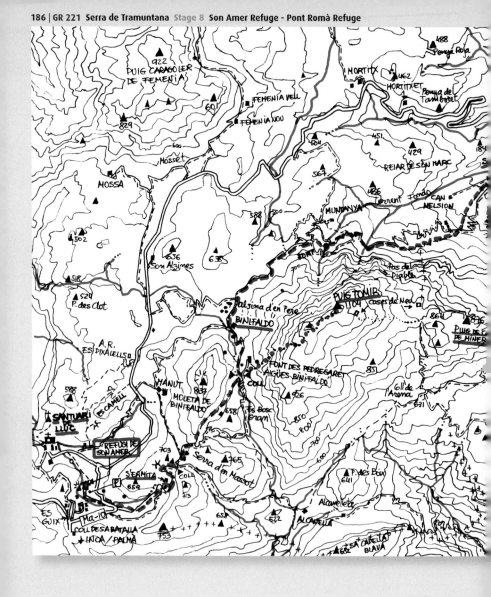

Map | 187

GR 221 STAGE 8	SECTION 8.1
	55 mins

FROM THE SON AMER REFUGE TO COLL PELAT

We leave Son Amer going down via a short cut with the sign, "GR 221 Pollença (4 h 45 mins). Caimari. Aparcament (car park)". Shortly, we link up with the path to the refuge, close to a washhouse and the canal of Font des Puig Ferrer. We approach the road and follow it for some 200 metres (we will have to cross it). We leave the road behind when we come to a signposted gate to the left. A little further on, we come out in the Camí de s'Ermita and we follow it on the left, in a calm ascent, until a nearby opening in a wall. Behind us we see the Son Amer refuge and the Mola d'en Galileu. Within the holm-oak wood, we cross a wide path and continue straight on in the same direction we are walking, towards the NE, along a narrow path that takes several bends.

The narrow path comes out to a crossing of tracks, but we continue in the same direction, to the bottom of the watercourse, where **S'Ermita** is hidden, modest and restored, surrounded

▲ **Canal of the S'Ermita spring**

by steep banks of cultivated land. It is thought to be dated from the 17th century and lasted until the 18th.

We walk SE to come to a climbing track that goes towards the Coll Pelat. We go as far as a lime kiln. After leaving two turnings to the right, after some 10 minutes climb, we find ourselves at another junction.

The path on the left with the sign "Mirador" (viewpoint), goes to a magnificent vantage point after about 400 metres,

▲ **Hermitage of Son Amer**

dedicated to the Mallorca Tourist Board. The viewpoint is situated on the crest of the Serra Mitjana, at an altitude of 670 m, and overlooks the entire Lluc valley.

The path on the right reaches Coll Pelat in a few minutes. The path borders, in the north, the estate of Son Amer.

▲ **Collier's hut**

GR 221 STAGE 8	SECTION 8.2 50 min.

FROM COLL PELAT TO BINIFALDÓ

▲ **Holm-oak wood of Binifaldó**

We go over the wall of Coll Pelat. We leave a turning to the right that goes towards the Alcanella valley. In a northwards direction, the flat way will take us to a new pass (686 m) where a track leads from our left and drops towards Menut, an old country estate, today public, where there are some forestry nurseries.

We, however, must continue along our way on the track on the right. Well signposted, it links up with Coll des Bosc Gran after 5 minutes walk. On the sign we see "Binifaldó 40 mins Pollença 3 h 40 mins".

The way goes along the hillside downwards to the bottom of the Es Bosc Gran watercourse. On the first sharp bend we must find a turning marked to the left. On an almost flat route, we cover the east side of the Moleta de Binifaldó (837 m) and in five minutes we reach a hill where the remains of an old woodcutters' hut are conserved. We will also have seen several huts and coal silos and the occasional oven. Accompanying us, in front, is the immense Puig Tomir.

In a half tour from Coll Pelat we reach Coll des Pedregaret, crossed by a strip of land with an opening. A new sign informs us of the closeness of Binifaldó.

We go through the opening and walk along an asphalted way that comes from the Ma-10 road and which leads to the bottling plant of **Font des Pedregaret**. The entrance to the plant is just to our right.

We continue on the road downhill, until the estate of Binifaldó, publicly owned and dedicated to environmental educational activities. The setting is ornamented by magnificent

▲ Puig Tomir

PUIG TOMIR

The county is dominated by the imposing Puig Tomir. The climb (optional), which may take 1 h y 30 mins, has two rather delicate parts.

The route up to the peak begins on the right, between the wall of the pass and the entrance to the El Pedregaret bottling plant. The path, winding and uphill continuously, initially follows a fence that is on our left. On leaving the wood behind, the path crosses a long pile of earth on its upper part.

Along a channel of rocks and with the help of a cable we reach a small hill. We move on to a second channel that we must also cross with the help of a cable and some iron steps. From here the climb, in NE direction, is less steep. After leaving to our left a first peak (1,083 m) we now see the higher peak of La Mola de Es Tomir, almost devoid of vegetation. The views are spectacular over the region of Lluc and over nearly all the north sector of the Serra. Some 200 m to the east, and at a

lower height, we will discover some buildings that will be familiar with us by now: the ice huts, made up of a porch for taking shelter, the snow well, where the snow was collected and compressed, and banks and walls that made it easier to collect. A path of hidden snow huts drops towards the Coll d'Es Puig de Ca.

examples of hundred-year-old holm-oaks and poplars and there are many springs.

The houses of Binifaldó are placed at the foot of the big Puig Tomir (1,082 m) of which we can see its imposing sides. A wide avenue opens up to the sown fields that surround the house. In the landscape we can see some of the neighbouring estates: Son Alzines, Mossa, Mosset, Femenia, among others. The irregular profiles on the horizon of the **Roig** and **Caragoler de Femenia** mountains dominate the panorama. To the east of the house there was a large plot of land. The name of the spot gives away its Islamic origins, transcribed Binihaldon, or sons of Haldum. In the *Repartiment* (sharing out) of the island of Mallorca, undertaken after the conquest of Jaume I, this part corresponded to the Order of the Temple. From the 15th century the property passed through different hands, until it was donated, in 1682, to the sanctuary of Lluc. Like the nearby estate of Menut, Binifaldó passed into state ownership in 1897.

▲ Fern

▲ Kite

GR 221 STAGE 8	SECTION 8.3 1 h 45 mins

FROM BINIFALDÓ TO PI DE SON GRUA

▲ **Binifaldó**

In the shadow of the tall poplars, a track leaves in a northerly direction that goes to the Collet de Binifaldó (598 m). We are now treading the Camí Vell (old way) from Lluc to Pollença. We come across some notable examples of holm-oak, such as the one called En Pere, always in a setting of typical undergrowth. There is no shortage of pine trees, either. Turtle doves and wood pigeons inhabit the high branches of the trees. Crows, kites, booted eagles and the occasional vulture fly over the spot. Like in all these woods of the Serra there are weasels, genets and martens, small predator mammals that are generally difficult to observe.

We pass an opening and continue through the wood. Remains of cultivated banks appear, of old smallholdings or signs of coal silos and collier huts. Through the pine trees and holm-oaks Puig Caragoler sticks out with its *ciurons* or *fics*, large rocks that form small isolated peaks, which char-

▼ **Holm-oak of En Pere**

acterise it. We go through another opening, which borders the large estates of Binifaldó and Muntanya. The landscape broadens and the way begins to go downhill gently. On our right stands the north face of Puig Tomir, with escarpments of 300 m. Opposite stand out the mountains of Pollença, dominated by Puig Gros de Ternelles (839 m).

The way becomes more winding. After leaving, on the left and right, two well-defined junctions, just past a sharp bend, we take the right-hand turning marked "GR 221 Pollença". After a quick descent in an eastward direction, a section of old bridle path, paved, takes us to the **Font de Muntanya**.

The water from the Font de Muntanya springs from a dry stone masonry vaulted spring, which forks into two springs. A canal takes the water to the houses of Muntanya. Some time ago, some benches and a stone table were built next to the spring. A solitary cypress tree remains. The corner of the spring, particularly during periods of rainfall, forms a very attractive pond, and is a great spot for relaxing. The country estate of Muntanya is removed from the route.

Just beside the stone bridge, we recover the **Camí Vell from Lluc to Pollença**, which we can shorten by taking different signposted short cuts, always going downhill.

We cover a flat section of the Camí Vell surrounded by woods. We go through an opening. On the first bend we leave it to continue straight along a straight, downward path.

The signs continue to show the way, until we come to one which at last says: "Pollença 2 h 30 mins". The way is winding and steep the whole time: but it soon becomes a track that drops along a watercourse. The large stones inform us of the closeness of the vertical buttresses of Fartàritx. To the left of the route we make out a rocky crest, made up of hills and *rellar* (abrupt extensions of limestone shaped by erosion).

▲ The *ciuró* of Puig Caragoler

▲ Lime kiln

▼ Valley of En Marc

We must continue in the same direction until coming to the Camí Vell again —now cemented. We continue taking short cuts, until the Camí Vell, now asphalted, takes us to the bank of the Torrent Fondo de Muntanya and to the fertile lands of the Vall d'en Marc. The estate of Son Marc, situated to the left of the way, conserves an oil press documented in the 17th century and an old garden. It is not visited.

The route runs between banks, almost always planted with fig, almond, apricot, pear and orange trees. There are water-wheels and wells that guarantee the supply of water. Small remnants of holm-oak groves and some riverside vegetation enrich the setting.

A sign, at the junction between the Camí Vell and the Ma-10 road, tells us: "Son Amer: 3 h 45 mins". The spot is known as Pi de Son Grua (km 5.3 / Ma-10). Very close, the Torrent de Son Marc takes shape, the joining of different streams that drain the mountains in these environs.

▲ Hawthorn (*Crataegus oxyacantha*)

▲ Mosses and polypody

8

FROM PI DE SON GRUA TO THE PONT ROMÀ REFUGE

▲ Façade of the refuge

We can make out to the north the powerful **Puig Gros de Ternelles**. Behind us we can recognise Puig Tomir, Puig de Ca and the Cuculla de Fartàritx, which extends in Pollença with the Serra de la Coma. The north side of the road creates a reduced valley, presided over by the houses of Son Grua, full of fruit trees.

We follow the road to our right, pass over a stone bridge and suddenly we leave the asphalt to continue parallel along the Camí Vell from Lluc. It is a section of track, shaded by the riverside wood, which accompanies the stream. To our side is an old canal in disuse. Shortly after we pass a small wooden bridge very close to the road, at km 4.85, facing the path that goes to Son Grua.

We turn again to the right of the route in order to follow another section of the Camí Vell. We leave a turning on the right, identified as Camí de Ca Llobera a la Torreta, while

▼ The old Roman bridge

our way continues straight on. Some 15 minutes from Pi de Son Grua we then, with the help of a small ladder, walk over a pile of dry stone masonry, full of pebbles that form a containing wall of the stream.

We continue along the left bank (along a section of uncared-for track broken up by the floods). We cross a path that links the road with the bank to the right of the stream and, after passing a gate, we reach the Ma-10 again.

Our route continues parallel to the road, until just before a ramp over a small stream that cuts the way, we provisionally turn towards the road, before Ca na Borrassa.

▲ **Pas d'en Barqueta**

Going north we will discover, on the side of the mountain, the old watermills of Llinars (today of residential use). The mills and waterfall that can be seen falling over the nearby rocky spot supply the Font de Llinars. Some of the mills are of Islamic origin. Other may date back to the centuries following the Conquest. There are seven constructions in all. Their former use was to grind flour or beat and prepare fabrics.

We go along a path next to the road until km 2.8 where a turning to the right (signposted) places us on an asphalted way, which we follow. Immediately, from behind the houses of Ca Pontico and on the left, comes an asphalted way from the road. We follow it towards the right: opposite, the hill of **Calvari** announces the closeness of Pollença and the right direction.

Between banks, we continue until a new contact point, on the left, with the road (km 2). By the Camí Vell, towards the right, we pass the stream over a footbridge. We are now in Pas d'en Barqueta. On the other bank, we turn towards the left, and between buildings and by the shade of the Calvari hill we reach the Pont Romà refuge, incorporated into the *Ruta de Pedra en Sec* in 2007. The Consell de Mallorca has rehabilitated the old slaughterhouse of the town built in 1908 to adapt it to its new use.

Puig de Maria ▶

8

CLIMB TO PUIG DE MARIA

Puig de Maria (325 m) is of natural and monumental interest, and is a beautiful variant epilogue of the Ruta de Pedra en Sec.

We will cross Pollença and close to km 52 of the Ma-2200 from Palma to Port de Pollença we come to the well-signposted path to the Puig. The climb, lasting 45 minutes, winding and very steep, climbs the northeast slopes of the mountain until passing the crag. The holm-oak, supported and protected by old banks, populates part of the route. After half an hour of climbing with bends, it reaches a point where what remains of the old way appears, paved and stepped that will take us to the flat peak where the monumental series stands of the Puig de Maria.

This small mountain overlooks an extensive panorama that takes in some mountains of the north part of the Serra (Tomir, Cuculla de Fartàrix, Puig Gros de Ternelles, Serra de la Font), the valleys of En Marc and Colonya, the bays of Pollença and Alcúdia, the flatlands of Sa Pobla, the marshy area S'Albufera and the distant ranges of Llevant. Tradition states that in 1348 an image of the Virgin Mary was found on this spot. It soon became a place of devotion, with the construction of an oratory and later founding of a community of nuns.

The oratory, remodelled in the 18th and 19th centuries, conserves traces of its old origins. A defensive tower and a fortified section surround the chapel and the adjoined buildings. Today it is a guesthouse, with a service of meals and accommodation.

**NATURE
NOTES**

Robin

Kestrel

Black vulture

**NATURE
NOTES**

Silo

Snow hut (Tomir)

Oven

Collier's hut

TOWNS

POLLENÇA

There are few towns in Mallorca where one can take part in so many demonstrations of popular culture as in Pollença. On Saint Anthony's Day (17 January), a huge pine tree is brought down from the wood of Ternelles, a country estate at the foot of the mountain of the same name, and in which stands King's Castle, the remains of a fortification from the times of the Christian Conquest of the island. For Easter, the procession of penitents fills the streets of the old centre and there is a performance of the spectacular *Davallament del Crist* (The descent from the Cross). For Corpus Christi and Saint John, the eagles of Pollença dance in the portal of the parish church. In summer, the entire town and thousands of visitors honour the Virgin of the Angels (2 August) with a full-blooded battle between "Moors" and "Christians", in memory of an attack of Turkish pirates to the town in the 16th century. In November, the *Fires* (fairs) offer objects for sale of the most varied local crafts (ceramics, fabrics, embroideries, cured meats).

Pollença is situated between two small hills: the Calvari, in the same town and with 365 steps that take you to the oratory that crowns it, and Mount María (325 m). The town is very lively and has all the services for both the local population and visitors. In the Plaça de la Almoina is *El Gall* (the rooster), the emblem of Pollença. Every Sunday the Plaça Major hosts the traditional market (crafts, vegetables, fruit). In Pollença you can attend concerts, visit art galleries, buy delicious local cakes, eat in renowned restaurants, visit the archaeology museum and Roman bridge, the birthplace of the poet Miquel Costa i Llobera (author of *Pi de Formentor*, perhaps the poet that best shows the character and symbolism of the Serra) or that of the painter Dionís Bennàssar, member of an aesthetic group known as the Pollença School of Landscapists. The setting of Pollença has places to visit that just cannot be missed. The Cove of Sant Vicenç, with the imposing range of

PRACTICAL GUIDE

Pollença Town Council
Carrer Escalonada Calvari, 2
07460 Pollença
Transports Illes Balears (Tib)
Tel. +34 971 17 77 77
http://tib.caib.es
Tourist information Office
Carrer Sant Domingo, 17
07460 Pollença
Tel. +34 971 53 50 77
oit@ajpollenca.net
Local information
www.ajpollenca.net

Pollença is a very lively town and big tourist attraction. It has all services and with a full commercial and cultural provision (museums, foundations, art galleries, cultural associations and philharmonic orchestra, etc.). It also conserves delightful traditions that coincide With the patron saint festivals (August) or with the Christian religious calendar (Easter, Corpus Christi and Christmas).

▲ **El Calvari**

▲ **Pollença market**

Es Cavall Bernat. El Cap de Formentor, with its lighthouse, from where you get views of some dizzying cliffs. The islet of Es Colomer, a spur in the sea, is a refuge for the dark endemic lizards and seagulls. The beach of Formentor is like a picture postcard. The port of Pollença centres the bay where the natural ornithological reserve of S'Albufereta is located.

REFUGES AND GUESTHOUSES

LA TRAPA (Andratx)
Not in operation at the time of writing.
Owned by:
Grup Balear d'Ornitologia i Defensa
de la Naturalesa (GOB)
Run by:
Consell de Mallorca

COMA D'EN VIDAL (Estellencs)
Not in operation at the time of writing.
Owned by:
Govern de les Illes Balears
Run by:
Consell de Mallorca

CAN BOI (Deià)
32 places. Dining room service.
Open all year.
Owned and run by:
Consell de Mallorca
Information and bookings:
Environmental Department
(Consell de Mallorca)
Tel. +34 971 17 37 00 / +34 971 17 37 31
Carrer General Riera, 111
07010 Palma (Mallorca)

MULETA (Sóller)
30 places. Dining room service.
Open all year
Owned by:
Ajuntament de Sóller
Run by:
Consell de Mallorca
Information and bookings:
Environment Department
(Consell de Mallorca)

Tel.: +34 971 17 37 00 / +34 971 17 37 31
Carrer General Riera, 111
07010 Palma (Mallorca)

TOSSALS VERDS (Escorca)
30 places. Dining room service.
Open all year
Owned and run by:
Consell de Mallorca
Information and bookings:
Environment Department
(Consell de Mallorca)
Tel. +34 971 17 37 00 / +34 971 17 37 31
Carrer General Riera, 111
07010 Palma (Mallorca)

SON AMER (Escorca)
52 places. Dining room service.
Open all year
Owned and Run by:
Consell de Mallorca
Information and bookings:
Environment Department
(Consell de Mallorca)
Tel. +34 971 17 37 00 / +34 971 17 37 31
Carrer General Riera, 111
07010 Palma (Mallorca)

LLUC (Escorca)
Rooms (129 cells for 1, 2, 4 or 6 people),
apartments, camping area and Sant Josep
refuge (26 places).
Restaurants and cafeterias. Food shops and
baker's. Open all year.
The Sanctuary of Lluc is not a refuge of the
GR 221, but a traditional centre of spirituality
and shelter in which mountaineers are always

welcome. You should book well in advance. Musum. Botanical garden. Information centre of the Serra de Tramuntana.
Owned and run by:
Missionaries of the Sacred Heart
Information and bookings:
+34 971 87 15 25
info@lluc.net
www.lluc.net

PONT ROMÀ (Pollença)
38 places. Dining room service.
Open all year.
Owned and run by:
Consell de Mallorca
Information and bookings:
Environment Department
(Consell de Mallorca)
Tel. +34 971 17 37 00 / +34 971 17 37 31
Carrer General Riera, 111
07010 Palma (Mallorca)

PUIG DE MARIA (Pollença)
60 places. Dining room service.
Open all year.
It is not a refuge of the GR 221. It is a hermitage (Hermitage of the Mare de Déu del Puig) with a traditional guesthouse.
Owned and run by:
Church of Mallorca
Information and bookings:
+34 971 18 41 32

CASTELL D'ALARÓ (Alaró)
30 places. Dining room service.
Open all year.
It is a refuge of the Ruta de Pedra en Sec.

It is an old rock-face castle with traditional guesthouse.
Owned by:
Alaró Town Council and Bishopric of Mallorca
Run by:
Fundació Castell d'Alaró
Location:
Municipality of Alaró
Information and bookings:
Tel. +34 971 18 21 12

NETWORK OF REFUGES OF THE CONSELL DE MALLORCA

Information:
www.conselldemallorca.net/mediambient/pedra

EMERGENCIES
Tel. 112

MOUNTAIN RESCUE
Tel. 085

FOR MORE INFORMATION

www.conselldemallorca.net
(Information about the Consell de Mallorca)
www.infomallorca.net
(Cultural and tourist information about Mallorca)
www.caib.es
(information about the Autonomous Community of the Balearic Islands)
www.illesbalears.es
(Cultural and tourist information about the Balearic Islands)

OTHER RECOMMENDED WEB SITES

Mountain Rescue Group **Grup de Rescat de Muntanya**
www.conselldemallorca.net
Balearic Federation of Mountaineering **Federació Balear de Muntanyisme**
www.fbmweb.com
Mallorca Hiking Group **Grup Excursionista de Mallorca**
www.gemweb.org
Balearic Ornithology Group **Grup Balear d'Ornitologia i Defensa**
and for the Defence of Nature **de la Naturalesa**
www.gobmallorca.com
Sanctuary of Lluc **Santuari de Lluc**
www.lluc.net

http://herbarivirtual.uib.es
(Information about botanic species in the Balearics)
www.ausdebalears.org
(Information about the birds of the Balearics)
www.cairesculturals.com
(The cultural aspect of Viatges Tramuntana and Grup Segall)